'An uplifting story about refusing to g[...] real inspiration to loads of people [...] backgrounds to Paolo.'

— Irvine Welsh

'[Paolo] offers rare insight into the psyche of those who grow up without the unconditional love of a parent.'

— *The Times*

'[Paolo's] experience as a writer is evident. Despite the emotional weight of the subject, *The Looked After Kid* is a pleasure to read.'

— *New Statesman*

'[Paolo] manages to offer insights and encouragement for cared-for youngsters – and their care staff.'

— *The Guardian*

'I cannot tell you how moved, touched, horrified and amused I was. I rate it with *Catcher in the Rye*.'

— Jilly Cooper

'An emotional book – it got to *me*.'

— Kevin Rowland, Dexys

'…the lack of journalistic gesticulation and presumption makes this both a refreshing and riveting read.'

— *Mojo* magazine

'On bookshelves packed with a growing genre of harrowing real-life stories, this book stands out… The book is well written, but his insight and self-awareness clearly come from a position that allows him to observe what he has experienced.'

— *Therapy Today* magazine

The Looked
After Kid

by the same author

But We All Shine On
The Remarkable Orphans of Burbank Children's Home
Paolo Hewitt
ISBN 978 1 84905 583 3
eISBN 978 1 78450 033 7

of related interest

No Matter What
An Adoptive Family's Story of Hope, Love and Healing
Sally Donovan
ISBN 978 1 84905 431 7
eISBN 978 0 85700 781 0

Shattered Lives
Children Who Live with Courage and Dignity
Camila Batmanghelidjh
ISBN 978 1 84310 603 6
eISBN 978 1 84642 254 6

The Looked After Kid

My Life in a Children's Home

Paolo Hewitt

Jessica Kingsley *Publishers*
London and Philadelphia

This revised edition published in 2015
by Jessica Kingsley Publishers
73 Collier Street
London N1 9BE, UK
and
400 Market Street, Suite 400
Philadelphia, PA 19106, USA

www.jkp.com

First published in 2002 by Mainstream Publishing

Library of Congress Cataloging in Publication Data
Hewitt, Paolo, 1958-
The looked after kid : memoirs from a children's home / Paolo Hewitt. -- Revised
[editioni]
    pages cm
ISBN 978-1-84905-588-8 (alk. paper)
1. Hewitt, Paolo, 1958-2. Foster children--Great Britain--Biography. 3.
Orphanages--Great Britain. I.
Title.
HV874.82.H49A3 2015
362.73'3092--dc23
[B]

2014017540

British Library Cataloguing in Publication Data
A CIP catalogue record for this book is available from the British Library

ISBN 978 1 84905 588 8
eISBN 978 1 78450 042 9

Printed and bound in Great Britain

For Dio, who gives me everything I need and then more, and
for S., who lives and breathes behind every word I write.
This book, it's all part of my way of giving,
just as you have given so much to me.

Contents

Acknowledgements

I want to thank my old agents, Julian Alexander and Lucinda Cook, for putting me on the right track when the first drafts of this book started emerging. I especially want to thank Bill Campbell at Mainstream for taking this work on initially. I also want to thank Mainstream's Fiona Brownlee and my editor Clive Hewat for the work they did on the original edition. I would like to deeply thank Stephen Jones and everyone at Jessica Kingsley Publishers for this reprint. I also want to acknowledge the hard work and talent that went into the book's many cover designs. Take a bow George Georgiou.

There are so many other people that I have to thank that I doubt I have the pages to name you all. But you know who you are. You came to me in the Home and you befriended me. You gave me cigarettes and companionship and you protected me from the fury of the bullies. You let me into your room and gave me wisdom and your body. When I left, you built a room for me in Aldershot which I never used and yet you never complained once. Your family took me in and I will never forget your kindness. You took all my money at cards but paid me back a million times over. So did your wife. You grinned and bore it when I smashed your rare olive oil. You kicked a car in Hackney and took my photo a million times.

I met you in London, the youngest DJ I ever knew, and then we played football in Hyde Park and swallowed the pill and chased girls together. You sang about solace and you sat with me on Camden High Street at five in the morning and held my hand. You never let me down, bald head, and you gave me the shirt off my captain's back, which still hangs upon my wall. We looked out for each other at the *NME* and I was proud to be in your first book. We smoked the ting and wrote our wayward favourite's story. We gave you the Chocolate Lady, you gave me Ali for my 40th. I watched you turn from a monkey to a man and watched all your family turn into angels. And I saw you go from disciple to leader.

You sat with me in Sorrento and gave me laughs and wisdom. When I arrived at your doorstep, you brought me into the family, made me feel so loved that tears would bubble in my eyes every time I left the Piazza Tasso. When I was ill you took me in and helped repair me. You sent me 'Some Kind of Wonderful,' which was wonderful, and you painted me *Heaven's Promise*. You brought us all together at Christmas and you burnt CDs in Birmingham. We reasoned a million times and we will reason another million. On a plane in Japan, tears dropped down your cheek when I told you my story and I will never forget those tears. And now it's all this. Fantastic, eh?

You know who you are and you know what you mean to me. And so for you, and for all the looked after kids everywhere – this one's for you.

One

The Walk

July 1958

During my second day on earth a nurse came and stole me from my mother. She walked into the ward where my mother slept, picked me up and carried me to a waiting car which then drove off into the black night. When my mother awoke she was without her third child, her first son.

I have wondered about that nurse many times. In idle dreams I have tried to picture her face, her body, her way of walking. Sometimes I have sought to place myself in her mind, to read the thoughts that raced through her head as she and I journeyed down that long and shiny-floored corridor. How did she feel? Was she sad? Did any regret at removing me from my mother's care find its way into her being?

How did she view me? With love? Hate? Disgust? If the truth be told it was probably with distaste. After all, the year was 1958 and I had been born a 'bastard' in a time when such a title carried huge shame. Two days old and already I lived without honour.

Maybe my daydreams do her a huge disservice. Maybe this nurse bore me no malice at all. Maybe she drew me in close and whispered sweet nothings in my ear, told me that everything would be all right even as she walked me to my fate. I wouldn't be surprised if she had. Those of us whose lives have been shattered forever always jump to the darkest of conclusions.

But there is one thing I would have liked to have asked her, one thing I have always wanted to know. Was she able to keep her eyes averted from mine? I mean from the time she picked me up to the time she lay me down? To this day I have no idea why the answer is so important to me. All I can be sure of is that this ghost in starch swept me away from my mother and threw me into the world. Yet I bear her no malice. On that day, 13 July 1958, she was only following orders.

In fact, she must have assumed that mother and son would never actually meet again; that I would be farmed out to someone or somewhere and there would be the end of it. After all, patients held in hospitals under the Mental Health Act, such as my mother, are not allowed to keep their babies. They never have been. And they probably never will.

And still I wonder about that nurse.

Two

Hurt Is Where the Home Is

April 1971

I wake up at a time you have never heard of and as always I wake up confused.

Did I open my eyes and then see staff member Maggie Paterson, arm raised, looming towards me, crying, 'Get up, get up!' or was it her shouting that shattered the dark I had just been inhabiting and forced me awake? This question kick-starts my every day in the Children's Home and I never bother to find the answer. Instead, I pull back the sheets and in my thin, striped pyjamas I step onto the thin carpet.

Paterson's angry words, 'Clean your face and teeth, right now,' burn my ears as I leave the room, turn sharp left and walk into the cold bathroom. There is a bare lightbulb above me and in front of the five sinks are two boys, heads bowed, energetically brushing their teeth. They spit out the paste with gusto. I see it splash against the sink, white on off-white. I move forward, shiver, and turn on the cold water. I splash my face, thinking of the actor Paul Newman who says he maintains his good looks by using cold water every morning. I read this in a recent interview although I am not that interested in the actor. My faves at this point in my life tend to be…

'Paul, wash your face! Standing there like a lemon!'

I wash face and teeth. The air is cold in here and there is dark outside. I too bend my head into the sink. Someone comes up next to me. I don't know who it is, nor do I care. I splash some more water on my face.

'Going to smash your face in today.'

Fuck. It is Mothy, standing there, strong, physical, his face exulting in the power that he knows is his to beat me with. He holds a toothbrush in his hand and he is jab-jabbing it angrily towards me. A shiver goes through my heart. My cheeks blush and I turn off the tap, move sharply away, never looking back.

In the bedroom I quickly change into my school uniform. Thankfully, Mothy sleeps in the upstairs bedroom so he can't reach me yet.

I pull on my trousers and notice the frayed material that covers my knees. If I fall over again at football today they will tear and then I will have to approach Maggie Paterson to ask for another pair. At which point she will shout and scream – wasn't I told not to play football on the school's concrete playground?

The shirt I button is thin and nylon, my tie grey and red. I hate my clothes. My friend's clothes at school are brand new, sharp-smelling and colourful. They wear tasselled loafers, Ben Sherman shirts and Levi Sta-prest. They are the latest fashion. My clothes aren't. Mine are cheap and shapeless and dull and next to them I feel like a pauper, although they never say anything about my clobber. Not like they do with other kids. Which is why I love my friends.

I push on my slippers. I go and stand in front of the mirror and pick up a hairbrush. Some mornings I hate looking at myself and today is one. I avert my eyes and brush my thick hair quickly. I put down the brush. Around me all the other boys are hurriedly dressing, all of them except for Stephen.

Stephen, seven years old now, sits on his unmade bed. As usual, he has a wide smile on his face. His hair is tousled, his eyes are alight. It's as if nothing can trouble him. I envy him. I grin and leave the bedroom praying I don't bump into Mothy coming down the top stairs. He has already beaten me up four times this week. As I leave the room, Barry Isleworth, the man in charge of the Home, comes out of the opposite bedroom wearing a dressing gown, grey and fluffy. His legs are white and hairy. 'The best in town,' he always boasts, 'the girls love them.' I find this hard to believe.

'Morning,' he says gruffly and he turns left and goes towards his bathroom. I follow him and when he goes in I carry on and enter the toilet. I close the door and urinate to the sound of Barry clearing his throat of last night's whisky and cigarettes. Time and time and time again, he retches.

It is a nasty sound but I have sympathy for him. I know what a bastard it is to give up fags. I've been trying since I was ten. Still, it doesn't stop me smiling at the sound of his discomfort. It feels like a kind of revenge. I dip and zip. I leave the toilet angrily roaring behind me.

I go past Barry and Julie's bedroom and descend the stairs. At the bottom, I turn right and walk into the dining room where breakfast is ready. The room contains four tables that sit six people each. My place is at Barry's table. Julie, his wife, sits at another with their daughter Belinda and some of the

other children. Maggie Paterson commands her own table. I
am so glad I don't have to sit with her. She reminds me too
much of my foster mum.

Thankfully, Barry has taken a shine to me and placed me
near him. I go over to the table by the hatch and pour myself
some cereal. I sit down at my usual place and within a minute
the cereal is gone. Milk marks my mouth. From behind me the
cook, Mrs Willoughby, puts her towelled head in the hatch
and shouts, 'Table two,' which means my hot meal is ready.
I'm first off the mark to the hatch. I pick up a plate carrying
two slices of bacon and four tomatoes and quickly return to
the table. I dab thin, white, margarined bread into the red
juice on my plate. Within two minutes, it is empty. Barry
now walks into the room wearing a pink shirt, grey trousers
which his stomach bulges over, a belt and white socks. He sits
shoeless at the head of our table and notices my plate.

'God's sake, Paulo, how many times do I have to tell you,
take your time with your food.' I don't know why he says
this. Mealtimes at the Home are not for talking and laughing.

If I have anything to say to one of the kids it is probably
best said out of earshot from the staff. If a staff member wants
to talk to me it will probably be a brief exchange because
they'll either be correcting me or commanding me or asking
questions to which I will reply in as short a manner as
possible. It's not that I dislike the staff – except for Maggie
Paterson, who always calls me Paul ('because that's your
name in English') – it's just that I may slip up and hand them
some information which will be used either against me or my
friends. Anyway, as my best mate in the Home, Jimmy B. says,
most of them will move on, so what's the point of talking to
them? 'They ain't nothing to us, are they?'

I look over at Mothy's table. God knows how long he
has been staring at me but now is his chance. He mouths

something to me. I only recognise the word 'kill.' Again, I blush; again, I look quickly away.

I watch Barry tucking into his cereal. I wish I could tell him about Mothy. I wish I could stop the beatings he is giving me. But I'm too scared to talk, to tell tales. Instead, I wait for Barry's nod so that I can leave the table.

'Who's on morning dishes?' Barry asks.

'Mothy and David,' Maggie Paterson sternly answers.

One will wash up, the other will dry. According to the rota, which hangs on the kitchen wall, my job today is maintaining and cleaning the boiler which I will do last thing in the evening. Other jobs include sweeping out the cloakroom, tidying up the playroom, hoovering the sitting room, sweeping the hall and stairs, washing out the porch and laying the tables in the dining room for teatime.

Because Mothy is on washing up I can now leave the dining room, go into the hallway, casually sneak the *Daily Mirror* off the sideboard, take it to the cloakroom, and read it in peace. It means I can scour the sports pages for any mention of my football team, Spurs, read the reports from last night's games and save Peter Wilson's sports column for last. All without having to worry about Mothy coming into the cloakroom.

Turning into a good day, this one.

I look at Barry and he nods his assent. I get up, put the empty plate on the hatch and leave, turning into the hallway and sweeping the *Mirror* off the sideboard under the stairs on my way. In the cold cloakroom, I read quickly, efficiently. Then I pull on my coat and shoes and leave by the back door.

I walk down the driveway in the dark, turn left and onto the road. In front of me lies roundabouts and hilly roads and large houses separated by tall trees and splashes of green. I live in Smalltown, Surrey. My school is about a mile and a half away and my journey always begins in morning blackness. I am fascinated by the dark. Every morning, I try to see where it magically disappears to.

Cars are already starting to choke up the road. From an open bedroom window, I hear a radio playing Paul McCartney's 'Another Day.' It amazes me how, after all these years, the man makes his music sound so effortless. I remember the first time I... A jolt hits me inside.

Shit.

I left the newspaper in the cloakroom. I didn't put it back on the sideboard in the hallway. Balls, balls and fuck. My negligence means that when I get home Maggie will give me a huge telling off. She will know it is me. She knows I'm the only one who avidly reads anything placed in front of me.

Worry hits me, starts surging to my brain, but that's no big thing. These days, I worry about everything. I worry that the fag I have just smoked will give me lung cancer. I worry about my looks, my weight, my clothes, my intelligence, my future, my friends, my everything. I worry about the Home and if it burns down what will happen to me. I even worry that Maggie Paterson is right and that I could well end up in prison if I am not careful. It is then that I think of my money hidden in the boiler room. I worry that someone will find it.

I turn into the long lane that leads up to our school. Dennis Harvey and a group of the boys from Highlands school are walking on the other side of the road. I put my head down, hoping they won't notice me. Highlands are our enemy. Their school is a mile away and sometimes there are skirmishes when we meet. Highlands are a lot tougher than us.

Walking with Dennis and his gang is a small kid of ten or eleven years. Probably someone's younger brother. I see the boys stop, whisper something in his ear and as I walk up the little boy crosses the road. He stops in front of me and he mumbles something. I stop and look at him.

'What?' I ask.

Again he mumbles. He's even more nervous than me. 'Sorry?'

'I said, do you want a fight?'

What a brilliant move. If I say yes, then they charge me and they beat me. If I say no, then they call me a coward and a chicken. And then they charge me and beat me. For the first time I notice how cold the morning air is today.

'Nah, mate,' I say, and I quickly brush past him. Then I start running. Behind me, a chorus of sneering voices erupt.

'Chicken.' 'Baptist bastard.' 'Wanker.'

I see Pete Garland up ahead of me and I sprint up and join him, glad to escape the taunts, the laughs.

'Wotcha,' I say, a little breathlessly.

'Wotcha,' he replies. The teachers hate us saying 'wotcha' to each other. 'Don't you know how to say hello to each other properly?' they ask us with real annoyance.

'Fucking Highlands boys nearly got me there.' 'They didn't notice me, the wankers.'

Neither of us are fighters. I am too weak and Pete is tall and skinny, very skinny. He has fair wavy hair and brown eyes. He is a tall boy who's great at football and puts us in stitches with his word-perfect renditions of TV adverts. Above all, his character is shot through with a very real and attractive kindness.

As usual, he carries his lunchbox under his arm. Through its plastic cover I can make out two layers of ham-and-tomato sandwiches. Pete will not eat them. We will. Stealing Pete Garland's lunch is now as much a part of our daily routine as lessons or assembly are.

The game is simple. When he arrives at school, Pete hides his sandwiches. We find them and then we eat them. Which is why Pete's nickname is Bones. He's that skinny. Also, he never flies into a rage when he discovers he has no lunch. He just laughs.

'You won't get them tomorrow,' he will state, an amusing look of mock determination upon his face.

Guess I am not the only one who wants to be liked.

Pete notices me looking at his lunchbox and casually switches it to his other hand.

He asks, 'Did you see *Monty Python* on telly last night?'

Damn. The Friday morning killer question has arrived and faster than usual. I am normally in school before it's first asked. Today I haven't even made it through the gates.

To my eternal shame, I can't watch *Monty Python*. I am not allowed. It is shown past my bedtime. But I can't tell my friends that. The embarrassment of them knowing that I have to go to bed at nine would kill me. It really would. Once, I half-heartedly enquired of Barry if maybe, just maybe, I could stay up one time to watch it. He chuckled.

'It's too adult,' he replied, 'and you have school the next day.'

Yes, I think to myself. And so do all my friends. Who aren't treated like little fucking kids. I imagine them at home, watching TV in warm sitting rooms with smiling parents. It's like missing out on a whole new world.

So every Friday I have to pretend that I forgot to watch it and in that very second, just as I am about to say it, that's when it really hurts to be a child in the Home, when I have to pretend that I can have what my friends have when I can't. For what my friends take for granted is the stuff of my dreams. That's because in my world if you don't watch *Monty Python* then you lose. Simple as that. You lose because you can't rush into school and act out a sketch and make everyone laugh. You lose because you can't sit there hoping that no one is going to act the sketch that you're saving up. You lose because you can't belong. My only relief is that at some point someone will change the subject to *Top of the Pops*. 'Anyone see T. Rex last night?' and then I'm in. 'Yeah, that "Hot Love" is great, been number one for three weeks now. Marc Bolan used to be acoustic and they weren't called T. Rex then, they were Tyrannosaurus Rex.'

No wonder I love music. You can listen to it before you get sent to bed. Unlike *Monty Python*.

'Oh shit, I forgot *Monty Python* was on,' I lie to Pete.

He takes a sideway glance at me. I see then that he knows the score. 'Yeah, it was good,' he says. He won't embarrass me by telling me every detail of last night's show and that's because of his kindness.

We walk along the pavement in silence for a bit until Pete decides to cover the space that has opened up between us.

'Double maths, today.' 'Fucking hate it.'

'And metalwork.'

'If he pokes me in the ribs again…'

'What about Doyle nearly giving us the cane?'

And Pete mimics our Deputy Head and maths teacher's catchphrase. 'I feel sure…'

We both laugh and connect and we pass through the school gates and head into the low-roofed building that is our school. When we arrive at the cloakroom, I see four dark blazers already hanging up which means that the morning game has already started. We shrug off our jackets and hang them up. Pete goes to the toilet. 'You go ahead, I'll catch up,' he shouts.

He is waiting for me to leave so he can hide his sandwiches.

I smile to myself, and head outside towards the playing field, crossing the concrete playground which is strangely empty and then onto the field where the smell of freshly cut grass hits me like a drug and makes me glide across the green carpet in front of me. The morning dew, scattered like jewels that very morning, illuminates my path to the game. 'Whose side?' I shout to the boys already playing. They look up. It is Vic and Tommy and the Bloan twins.

'You're with us,' Vic says, 'Pete's on theirs.'

The ball is passed to me, I control it and move forward. In the distance are more fields and placed on their edges are the little houses. Occasionally I stand and try and visualise the lives that go on in them. Are they like mine or are they normal? Behind me are the white school buildings and the boys' and girls' playgrounds, divided by a patch of land and wire fences. Over to my left is the tiny golf course built by Mr Cosgrave, the Head, and it is there I will smoke my first joint with Dave McGinty, the school hippie.

In front of me, as I run with the ball, my friends wear faces of real studied concentration, expressions you would never see in any of our classes. They are watching me, watching the ball, and I am just so happy to be here, to forget Python, to forget Maggie Paterson, to forget a past which is broken into jigsaw pieces, forget it all and get lost in a game played in the morning of a magical world.

For twenty minutes we play. By the end, my side is winning.

'We win, eleven–nine,' I shout as we hear a bell ringing in the distance. 'No, it's not,' shouts Billy Bloan, one of the twins. 'We've got ten goals.' He has the ball and wants to score a quick one. That won't happen. I rush over to tackle him.

'Fucking haven't,' I shout as I place myself in front of him. He's not good enough to get past me.

'Balls,' he shouts, jerking his body, trying to fool me into going the wrong way.

'He's right, it's only nine,' Pete shouts over and as he is on Billy's side that settles the question. The bell rings again and we look to see the figure of Mr Deish walking towards us. Vic runs over, picks up the ball from Bloan's feet and all of us start jogging towards the school. Assembly, taken by the headmaster, will start soon and it is not advisable to get there late. 'Morning, sir,' we shout as we pass Mr Deish. Already, I am looking forward to break time and starting another game. Billy Bloan won't be on my side, that's for sure.

'Hey, hey, hey,' Mr Deish shouts at us, 'you're not going into assembly like that. Look at you. Do yourselves up. You look like tramps.' 'Yes, sir.'

We stop, straighten ourselves up, brush the green that's burnt into our arms as Mr Deish, portly in a blue shirt, impatiently watches us. Then he curtly nods his approval and turns away from us. We turn as well, walk through the nearest door, turn left and bang! – my heart adds a beat. She is here. Despite the fact that there are children everywhere around us, that there are boys laughing and there are girls chatting, all I need is a glimpse of that shiny hair and I am floored.

Today she is wearing a skirt made out of Trevira material, white tights, buckled shoes, a blue jumper that covers her blue shirt and school tie. Her breasts point out like little pears. I often can't bear to look at them.

Billy Bloan says, 'We did have ten goals,' but I don't care now, I really don't.

I have been in love with her for three years now and at some point I really should talk to her. I am desperate to know how she thinks. I want to know about her life and her family. I want to tell her how I feel and I want more than anything in this world for her to be my girlfriend. It would make me feel so proud, so grown up. But every time she comes near the words from my heart get caught in the lump in my throat because I am scared, scared to death that she will laugh at me and say don't be so silly, how can you take me out on two shillings a week pocket money, how can you take me out when you have to be home by (short laugh) nine? Tell me that.

To hear those words would kill me. So I love her from afar because it is so much safer that way. I walk towards the assembly hall with my eyes trained on her back, oblivious to the noise around me. The words of my friends, the chatter of the mass, are nothing to me. The world has vanished into that shiny dark-brown chestnut hair.

I walk into the assembly hall in a state of pure love. Three hundred children sit on red chairs which face a raised stage and one by one they fall silent. Behind the stage is a large window that looks out onto the school's forecourt where the teachers park their cars. A row of them, young and old adults, now sits and faces us. There are white-haired teachers and fat teachers. There are long-haired teachers and there are suited teachers. There are ugly teachers and middle-aged women. Then there is Miss W., the girls' PE teacher, in her usual dress of a short maroon skirt, her brown legs firmly crossed, warning off all the boys' eyes.

Beneath us is a shiny wooden floor.

'Fucking was ten goals,' Billy Bloan hisses at me.

The teachers glance to the right and all of us stand as Mr Cosgrave, the Head, walks out onto the stage. Mr Cosgrave is a small, Scottish man who always wears a tweed suit covered by a black robe. His face is clean-shaven, his hair short, severe. His reputation as a man of stern principles is so much taller than he is.

He nods and we sit down again. A pointless ritual. Life is full of them at this age. Mr Cosgrave places his papers on the lectern in front of him and then considers us with the air of a man already disappointed by a wrapped gift he has just been given.

'The netball team,' he announces in his Scottish accent, 'lost 14–4 to Highlands School yesterday. Half-term will start this year on 21 April. It will last a week. The trip to...' His Scottish accent has been diluted by Surrey air and water.

My mind wanders, so do my eyes. I try and locate where she is sitting. Next to me, Enzo Esposito is making the 'wanker' sign very slowly at Vic who has his tongue placed in his cheek.

'...the school will be holding a jumble sale this Saturday...'

I crane my head slowly backwards and spot her watching Mr Cosgrave. If she knows I am looking she is doing a good job of ignoring me. I look back at Mr Cosgrave and just as I do, outside on the forecourt, a police car suddenly glides into view. For a couple of seconds a palpable shiver of excitement and wonderment shoots through us all. We quickly flick each other with eyes and elbows.

Two stern-looking officers with helmets on get out. They are wearing white shirts and tiny blue radios, that look as much part of their body as anything else, are pinned to their chests. They look slightly ridiculous. They slam shut their car doors and right on the beat I hear Mr Cosgrave say, 'And I want to see Paulo Hewitt and Lazlo Molnar in my office straight after assembly. Mr McSherry will now take prayers.'

They have caught us. I don't know how but we have been caught. Someone must have split on us. How else could anyone know? I haven't said a word to anyone about the robbery and I am sure Laz hasn't either. I feel a numbness freeze my face. I have to find out. I look over at him.

Laz is sitting down the end of my row. He is staring straight ahead. His face too is covered in red. Mr McSherry announces, 'The Lord's Prayer,' and the entire school stands and begins to chant.

'Our Father / Who art in Heaven / Hallowed be thy name / Thy kingdom come / Thy will be done / On earth as it is in Heaven…'

I look over again at Laz, who now looks at me and raises his eyebrows in a slightly comical manner. I realise that he has decided not to care at all about what is about to happen.

'Give us this day / Our daily bread / And forgive us our trespasses / As we forgive those who trespass against us.'

I remain quiet, nerves and worry building in my stomach.

'And lead us not into temptation / But deliver us from evil… Amen.' (Oh, how I wish.)

We cross ourselves and everyone now stands. I remain sitting until I can find the strength to stand on empty legs. Laz now sidles up to me.

'How do they know?' I ask him.

'I don't know,' he replies. 'Ain't got a clue. Might not be about that anyway,' he says with real nonchalance.

Laz is hard, Laz is tough. I often wished he lived at the Home. Then Mothy wouldn't be able to make my life hell. Laz would murder him.

'Someone has split on us,' I say.

'Kill the bastard if he has,' Laz replies. His calmness amazes me.

We start the silent walk to the Head's office. We pick our way through the chairs and come out of the assembly hall. We go through the cloakrooms where a few kids are busy talking and gibbering and laughing before class begins. They see us but try to pay no attention. I can feel their eyes on my back, though. We enter the school's busy hallway and turn right into Mr Cosgrave's secretary's office. He is not ready to see us yet. His secretary tells us to wait. We do so in silence, gazing at the plain brown carpet at our feet. We ignore his secretary, the white-haired, bespectacled and very corpulent Mrs Davies, who busies herself at her desk, humming a tune under her breath. I try to recognise it but can't concentrate enough because through the door I can hear muffled voices and they are plotting our fate. Laz looks up and gives me a little smile of encouragement. I do the same to him but half-heartedly. Feelings churn unstoppably in my stomach. Questions fly at me like hungry bats.

What happens to me when Barry is told? In my mind's eye I see him shouting at me. I see him screaming. I see him viciously wagging his finger just before my nose. I see him furious, maybe so furious that I will be thrown out of the Home? Then what? Where will I go then? Another Home? Another school? Yet another beginning to go through until that ends and I start all over again once more?

Laz is all right. He lives with his mum. She dotes on him and his brother. I've been round to his house, I've seen it, envied it. Somehow, she will make him feel like it is all their fault and nothing to do with him. Not my little boy – oh no.

The door to our left opens. Mr Cosgrave peers gravely at us for about three seconds. With his finger he motions for us to come in. My stomach drops to another level, one I never knew existed inside me. Laz and I walk into his small office. As we do so, Cosgrave walks back to his brown desk. He sits and looks the pair of us straight in the eyes.

'This is Paulo Hewitt and Laz Molnar,' he says to the policemen who are facing him. The uniforms turn round in their chairs and examine us. I don't look at them. I stand with my hands behind my back.

Cosgrave's fingers start tapping on the desk. Outside the empty police car glowers at us. The policemen look at us with interest. They have their helmets on, which squash their faces and make them look stupid. They don't care. Their eyes tell me that they are thoroughly enjoying the game.

'I am going to ask you just once,' Cosgrave says, 'if you were the two who were involved in a robbery that took place at the local football ground three weeks ago. Well?'

Laz and I stand in silence. So nervous are we, we don't understand that he has already asked the question.

'The problem you have, boys,' interjects the policeman sitting nearest to me, 'is that someone overheard one of you boasting about this crime.' 'It was you,' Cosgrave says as a matter of fact, 'and no point in the denying of it, eh?'

I am far too shaken up to talk but Laz has gathered himself.

'Yes, sir,' I hear Laz say in a tone so good-natured it's as if he was admitting to a good deed done rather than to the crime in question. 'It was us.'

'Hewitt?' Cosgrave asks, ignoring my friend's pure cheekiness. 'Yes, sir, it was us.'

'I really didn't expect any different,' he says.

The second policeman speaks. 'As you have admitted to the crime your parents need to be informed. We are here to take you home but first Mr Cosgrave wants words with you, that's right, isn't it?'

Cosgrave nods his head. I notice the gel that tightly holds his hair down and makes it wet and shiny like a fish's body.

'We'll be in the car. Waiting.' They stand and walk past us, leaving us alone with Cosgrave. He stares at us for a few seconds and then twists in his chair to consider us from another angle. I see he has on a pair of bogus tan brogues. They are not made by Frank Wright, the type my friends all wear. It would feel so wrong if they were.

'I am very much of the opinion,' he begins in a low, intense voice, 'that the pair of you should be expelled for this matter. I will not have thieves in my school at any time. To steal is the most despicable of crimes. To rob people of their hard-earned money. The man you took fifty pounds from, did you know him?'

'No, sir,' I quickly say. I don't want Laz replying and pushing Cosgrave any more than he already has with his insouciant tone.

'He has a wife and two children. Did you know that?'

'No, sir,' I say.

'He works, works hard, supports his family. He isn't rich. Fifty pounds pays for a lot of things. Like food on the table, bills, holidays, things for his kids. And you two boys come along and take all that from him.'

Cosgrave glares at us but Laz and I can't look at him. We stand, hands clasped behind our backs, looking out onto the forecourt where the policemen have now settled in their car, which in turn seems to glower at us. 'Hewitt,' Cosgrave suddenly snaps, 'your teachers tell me you show some promise. They say you have a brain. Does this brain of yours ever tell you that behaviour like this is evil, a sin against God? Eh?'

'Yes, sir,' I dutifully reply.

'Others give you leeway because of your unfortunate circumstances but I don't. I don't think not having a family gives you the excuse to act like a villain. Do you?'

'No, sir.' My voice sounds weak. I hate its tone of subservience.

But at least he doesn't regard me with the loathing that he now looks at Laz with.

'Molnar, you've been a no-good waster all your life and you always will be. One day you will go to prison. Of that I am certain. I take it you were the instigator behind this.'

He hates Laz. Not because Laz doesn't read books or do his homework. But because Laz doesn't care that he doesn't read books or do his homework.

'Yes, sir, it was me behind it. My idea,' Laz brightly admits. I feel a shiver of warmth for my friend's gesture.

'You are both suspended from school until further notice. Go and get all your belongings and leave the premises. I will be informing your parents and [he nods at me] the Home of my decision as to whether you are to be expelled. Go now,' he says, waving his hand as if brushing a fly from the lapel of his tweed jacket.

'Yes, sir.'

We walk out, back through the outer office and into the school's main hallway.

Both of us turn towards the cloakroom and Laz says, 'Fucking hell, Jock Cosgrave forgot to give us the cane,' and he giggles. I remain quiet, serious. For the first time I feel the enormity of what we have done and the situation I am in. If I'm expelled then I will lose that which is most valuable to me: my friends. No more hanging out with them all day long, playing football, taking the mickey, laughing, feeling good. On top of that, it has shocked me – really shocked me – to discover that there is someone who would split on us. I always assumed everyone liked me. Always. Being the kid in the Home, I thought, gave me protection. I am without parents. Who would dare harm the orphan? I now know the answer. Plenty of people, plenty.

'I am going to fucking find out who split on us,' Laz says, 'and I am going to smash that bastard in. You watch.'

Laz takes on anyone, even if they're a year above him, he doesn't care. He never backs down. He wades in, takes the punches but gives them back with equal measure. But I don't care now about revenge. All I care about is what happens next.

We get our blazers and walk out to the waiting police car. This is the first time I have ever been in a police car. I feel as if I am a silly boy in a man's world gone wrong. Criminals travel in police cars. The kind of criminal that Maggie Paterson keeps telling me I will become. Normally, I would laugh every time she flew into such a tirade. I would laugh inside and think, what a ridiculous woman you are. But today I had started to prove her words right. Who's ridiculous now? We get into the back seat and the car moves off.

'Silly thing to try and pull off, wasn't it lads?' the policeman who's driving says casually as we pass through the school gates. 'Next time, you might try and keep your mouths shut when you're boasting to your friends about how tough you are.'

'Except there won't be a next time,' the second policeman interjects, turning in his seat to view us, 'because from now on we will be keeping an eye on you two.'

I sit and stare out of the window. I realise that I live nearest so I will be the first to be dropped off. The only sound in the car is the crackle of voices that burst intermittently through the radios.

The car wends its way towards the Home. More silence. Laz and I sit opposite, looking out of our respective windows. The car takes a right and pulls up the driveway to the Home. To my horror, Barry is already standing by the front door. He is wearing a pair of lime-green socks. I wonder where his shoes are.

I get out of the car and walk towards him. The driver of the car gets out as well. Barry refuses to look at me.

'Hello, officer,' Barry says brightly.

'Good morning, sir. Little present for you,' he says, nodding at me. Then his voice becomes serious and police-like. 'At some point we will be needing statements from these two so we will be in touch very soon. Okay?'

'That's fine, officer.' 'Good, see you then.'

The policeman walks back to the car and as he opens the door he pulls a face at me that says, well, what can I do about it? This is all your own fault. The car starts up again. Laz doesn't look back at me or wave goodbye. All I see is the back of his head. I wonder if I will ever see him again.

Barry, still watching the car turn round, hisses at me, 'Get upstairs to your bedroom now and don't you move an inch until I get there. You are in very big trouble.'

I go into the hallway, turn left and walk up the stairs to my bedroom, one by one by one. I turn left on the landing and go and sit on my bed. It is so strange to be here in this empty room at ten in the morning. I rarely see my bedroom like this, a row of beds with just silence sleeping in them.

I lie down on my bed. Suddenly I am exhausted, whiplashed by a day I wish I had never awoken to meet. It was all so unexpected. So sudden. There had been no alarm bells, no warning signals. No one cried, 'Watch out, big trouble coming your way.' No one made a sound. It was a glimpse at the chaos that lives underneath us all. How life can fool you into thinking that you know its nature and its character and then bang! leap out at you like an angry jack-in-the-box.

Downstairs, I hear the front door crash loudly. Then silence, nothing but a wary uneasy silence. I lie on my bed and I look at the ceiling. I feel hollow, empty.

I wish I could be at school right now. I wish I could be bored out of my mind, struggling with some maths sums in class right now. I wish I could hear Mr Sexton say, 'You know, Paulo, if you paid as much attention to this subject as you do the pop charts then you might get somewhere.' I wish I could be looking out of the window at the sports field and dreaming of football. I wish She was sat in front of me and I could lose myself in the shiny sea that is her hair. I wish I could be anywhere but here right now.

My mind doesn't want to think about what is coming. So it runs away, reverses itself and stretches itself back to the night Laz and I robbed the football club. Again, I see myself talking with him and his brother Sam, and again I see that mischief dancing in Laz's eyes that night, like a radar screen gone crazy.

It was a Tuesday and we are at the local youth club, bored, listless. We go outside for a cigarette – that is me, Laz and his brother Sam. As we flick flames towards our mouths, Laz notices the floodlights at the local football ground turned full on. The night clicks alive.

'Well, look at that,' Laz remarks and we all turn to see the lights that stand about two hundred yards away, blazing into the dark. No one says a word, no one makes a noise, but the lights have set something extraordinary in motion.

All of us follow the team, all of us know their fixtures inside and out. They are not playing tonight, so why are the floodlights on? The lights grow as big as the moon and, as if in a trance, we begin walking towards the ground. Nothing has been said but something has been transmitted. I just don't know what it is yet. Sam does. He smells something and it stops him in his tracks. It makes him shake his head and back away from Laz and me.

'No,' he says, 'no, I'm not doing it.'

I don't know what he is talking about. I don't know what we are going to do. Sam turns, walks away, back towards the youth club. Laz looks at me. I look back. That's it. It is decided. We carry on to the end of the road where we turn right and walk up to the ground, our pace subtly slowing.

'I think they must be training,' Laz muses. Of course. Hadn't thought of that one.

In front of us is a gravel car park coloured by light and dark shadows. There are a few cars parked here and there. A purple Morris Minor, a dark-green Ford Escort, a white Volkswagen Beetle, a very dark-blue Vauxhall Viva. Across the gravel are the turnstiles and to the left of them is the main entrance. Again, not a word, we just slowly walk towards the wooden door marked 'Entrance,' our feet digging deep and noisily into the weak gravel. The noise doesn't worry me. If anyone asks we will tell them that we thought there was a game on, that's all.

We reach the door. Laz puts his finger to his mouth. I nod. I still don't know what I am doing. But I do. Laz pulls back the door and we enter the club's hallway.

There are three doors in front of us and the walls are painted a dirty white. Laz nudges me, gestures towards the door which has 'Changing Room' splashed in red on it. We go towards it. Laz takes the silver handle and pushes down slowly on it.

The door gives and opens up slowly to reveal two benches stood in the room's centre, hooks on the grey walls and all the players' clothes hanging there like deflated scarecrows. Laz whispers, 'Keep a lookout. Guard the door.'

He walks into the changing room; I follow. I stand behind the door but keep it slightly open so I can see into the hallway. I am in a kind of trance now. Laz starts putting his hand into various trouser pockets. Shirts with big collars hang limp on top of these trousers and coloured ties hang upon them like ribbons. His hand slips into corduroy, linen, denim and cotton. I look behind me. Clear. I look back. Laz is on his tiptoes, trying to reach into another pair of trousers.

Give us this day our daily bread and lead us not into temptation.

He glances over at me, his arm in a loop, his hand looking as if the material has grabbed him. Then he looks at me, his eyes shining and pulls out…a handkerchief. He makes another 'shhh' noise and stuffs it back into a pocket. Laz is almost laughing with fear. He turns and considers the clothes hanging above the wooden benches. He has a ruddy face, Laz, and curly hair and small eyes and a smile that reaches his eyes and makes him irresistibly cheeky.

Come on! I am screaming to him from inside, come on, get a move on. Then his eye spots something. He reaches up and he pulls out a lumpy, black wallet. He opens it, and stares for a second; then he looks at me triumphantly, like this is the moment he has been waiting for all his life.

He stuffs the wallet in his back pocket and whispers, 'Fucking hell, let's go.' He pushes past me and as he does I smell his excitement. I close the door softly and we tiptoe across the floor, like two drunk ballet dancers.

We pass through the main door and onto the car park. At every step we take, the gravel beneath us roars like a volcano. Every heartbeat sounds like a jackhammer. I follow Laz and our footsteps pick up speed. I daren't look behind us. I keep waiting for a voice to shout 'Oi, you!', but the only noise is made by us, our thunderous and ominous walking on splintered, coloured gravel.

We reach the main gate but instead of heading back to the youth club we cross the road in front of us and turn right. We walk quickly up the curved road and turn into an alley on the left-hand side which leads onto another playing field. We stop in this small alley, breathless, high and dizzy.

'Fucking hell,' Laz shouts.

He opens up the wallet and he pulls out fifty pounds. I have never been near such a large amount of money in my life. Nor has he.

'Fucking hell,' he keeps saying, 'fucking hell.'

He is smiling and looking at the money, pulling it out, counting it and rejoicing. But me, I live a shattered life so I am already looking on the dark side, already thinking, what exactly am I going to do with this money?

For all the while, it has been dawning on me that although I crave money for clothes to look like my friends, this money is absolutely of no value to me. I can't go to the local boutique and buy a lovely pair of Frank Wright loafers or a crisp Ben Sherman shirt or a Crombie coat. How can I? Straight away, someone at the Home will demand to know where those brand new clothes came from and how I got the money to pay for them. And I won't have an answer – just resentment that whatever you do as a looked after kid, whether it is good or whether it is bad, there will always be someone asking you questions about it. Always.

It strikes me hard but I have just put my life on the line for absolutely nothing. Laz hasn't got that problem. He doesn't have to explain anything to anyone. In fact, the next day he will go the local café and eat the biggest breakfast ever placed in front of a boy and pay for it proudly. Right now, though, he is fired up, dancing inside with joy. I cannot enjoy the moment although I pretend to and say 'fucking great,' and go to put my arm around Laz's shoulders and say 'fucking great,' but all the time I feel awkward and hate myself for having to act out yet another character. 'Right,' Laz says, handing me fifteen pounds in large, blue fivers (although it might as well be a foreign currency for all the good it will do me), 'this is your share. Let's split up now, go home before anyone sees us. The best thing, yeah?'

Then his face splits into two as he cracks open that huge smile again. 'Fucking hell,' he goes, 'look at that.'

He takes another look at the money he is clutching and then stuffs it in his pocket. We move off and split up at the bottom of the alley. I go right; he goes left. I walk past the football ground. The lights are on, the car park is half lit; the cars are still waiting. I half expect someone to reach out and grab me. I walk quickly towards home. For no reason whatsoever, I keep thinking someone is watching me. I keep looking back behind me, keep expecting to be caught.

Finally, I get to the Home. I walk halfway up the driveway and then turn left. Now I am heading towards the back of the building. On the way, I stop and pick up a large stone. I reach the outside boiler room and peer down the stairs. No one is there. Good.

I tiptoe down the stairs and enter the small room. The heat fills my head. The smell of coal fills my nostrils. I put down the stone, and fish out the fifteen pounds which has been burning my leg with its own particular heat through my pocket since I took it. I go behind the boiler, kneel down and place the money carefully on the ground. Then I go back, get the coal dust-scarred stone and place it on top. I stand up, check again that nothing looks suspicious, then come back up the stairs. From the light of the house I can see how dirty my hands are.

I go into the cloakroom, turn on some water and stand by the sink washing my hands. I think I am cleaning them. In fact, I am trying to erase sin from my soul. I go to bed, quickly.

For the next three weeks I make visits to my money. I look at it, make sure it is still there, then I leave it alone. I have no idea what to buy with it. I am determined not to arouse suspicion. I don't even buy cigarettes with it in case the shopkeeper demands to know what a young boy like me is doing with a five pound note. Even I am in awe of how vast a five pound note is.

I still hadn't moved the money by the time we got busted.

* * *

Now, at least, I can pay my share back. That will be something. I can go to the... I hear footsteps on the stairs and then a loud, bitter voice.

'Paulo, get yourself down here, right now. I want to talk to you.'

My appointment with Barry Isleworth has just arrived. As I walk towards him, I think bitterly to myself, Paul McCartney is wrong. So wrong. It wasn't just another day.

Afterwards – after he has ranted and shouted and screamed and placed his face so near to mine that tiny drops of saliva splattered me as he asked me if I knew the man I had stolen from, and did I think he was rich or something to take his money, his hard-earned money and food from his kids' mouths, and was I always led astray so easily, is that how weak I was, and what kind of person did I want to become, did I really want to become a criminal because if that was what I wanted then I was going the right way about it, and there were all these people who had done so much for me and I had let them down, and not only that, I had let myself down, and so I would not be allowed out of the grounds until Barry said so, and I would pay back every penny that I stole and I better pray that I am not expelled...after he had said all that, I go to Jimmy B.'s bedroom and I pick up his mattress and find what I had been thinking about the whole

time Barry was raging at me: a packet of slightly flattened
Number Six cigarettes and a box of matches.

Jimmy will go mad at me for nicking them, but I can deal
with him when the time comes. He might just understand.
I leave his room and softly make my way downstairs. I hear
Barry in the sitting room talking to Julie. They're talking
about me. The house is devoid of children so their voices
sound louder than usual. I can smell cabbage coming from the
kitchen. It is a sickly smell and reminds me of school. I wish
it didn't. I really do.

I don't bother to listen to their conversation. I know it
already. Barry has told me to stay in my bedroom until further
notice but I have other plans. I skip across the hallway, into
the playroom and find my way outside. Three hours earlier I
had been playing football in thin sunlight. Now darkness half
covers the sky and a black wind begins to pick up. Normally, I
would smoke in the boiler room, the safest and warmest place
to hide. Today, I don't care. I stand at the top of the stairs in
the small courtyard and I pull out the matches as well as the
crumpled green-and-white Number Six box from my pocket.
I open it and six brown-and-white missiles reveal themselves
to me. I take one out, fire it up. I smoke quickly, with a touch
of desperation. I shiver against the wind which is cutting into
my nylon shirt. I suck hard on the smoke. Blow and suck.
Then I throw the ciggy down on the ground, squash it against
the steps. I draw out another ciggy, fire it up, puff heavily
upon it. Soon it's gone. Good. I smoke another. Now another.
I could get caught at any point but I don't care.

I glance up at the sky again. Grey clouds of unrelenting
depth hang above me as I take more smoke into my lungs.
I extinguish my fourth and light my fifth. I take a drag and
cough. A small ball of lime-green matter pops into my mouth.
I spit it out and it lands yards away from my feet. I stamp

out my ciggy. I feel sick and dizzy now so I go back inside, silently retracing my steps to my bedroom. Barry and Julie are still talking about me in urgent whispers.

I strip off my school clothes and stand in my underwear. I climb into bed, pull the sheet and two grey blankets over my head and dive into the darkness. All I want now is oblivion. It soon comes.

The fever arrives, vicious in its nature. My temperature begins to rise: 99, 100, 101…and as it does so I feel myself slipping away into new spaces, deep dimensions where faces loom in front of me, some strange, some not. There is Barry's face, his beard made wet by spittle, shouting silent words. There is Cosgrave's face up-close, tight and bulging with anger and then a face I do not recognise takes its place. I stand dumb in its presence until the most powerful force I have ever encountered sweeps me up from behind and hurls me towards a malicious presence. Suddenly I hear a scream. Long and loud. Purple clouds clear in front of me. I look down to see two young children laughing. Shouting. Running through a square packed with people. The boy chasing the girl. The pair of them zig-zagging into an alleyway. Running fast. Running carelessly. Running finally into a woman who is placing fruit in a basket that is tied to a rope hanging down from a small window. Apples, pears, oranges now spill out onto the pavement. They roll away from her, bumping against the cobbled streets she walks each day. Bruising them forever.

And the woman I know. For the woman is my mother.

Three

It's The Good Life

Sorrento, Italy, 1947

I really hope that at some point in your life you get to hear the waves that lap the Sorrento coastline, gently sucking out the last gasps of breath from the forever stones that lie on its beaches. My head is filled with this wondrous sound as I lie upon the small wooden pier that pushes out uncertainly into the languid sea. Above and beyond, the air hangs still and on either side of me small fishing boats rock from side to side, dark nets slung carelessly over them. On both sides of the bay, green luxuriant hills think they are mountains and push lazily towards the clouds. Tiny villages breathe happy on their brow. To the left of me I hear a slow engine start up, ready to take the people to the small island of Capri which lies to the west. And there, stood proud inside the tranquillity known as the Bay of Napoli, Mount Vesuvius stands aloof, a brooding, imperious presence, swathed as ever in mist.

It is in such a setting, vast and soulful, that I want to lose myself. For this is where it all began, in Sorrento, the home of my mother, this magical town, permanent and sacred where, in children's faces, Sorrento people glimpse God and are given a purpose. ·

But my mother lost hers. She gave it away to love.

Eyes flash, eyes lock and love sparks into life for the fifteen millionth time that day, another small eruption in the world. This love begins in Sorrento's Piazza Tasso, where at night the people dress up and parade themselves, creating the eternal procession that is the heartbeat of the town.

The Piazza Tasso is where my mother and father looked at each other for the very first time. Their hearts didn't so much skip a beat as gain a few. He was English, a soldier, stationed near Napoli; she was a local and strikingly beautiful. War was over now for both of them. His unit had stayed on with other soldiers, mainly Americans, there to ensure, in the name of democracy, that no one voted for the Communists. My mother was nineteen but she was also tired. She lived with her two brothers, Gio and Antonino, over their grocer's shop where she worked and she cleaned and she cooked and she worked and she cleaned and she cooked. Much was expected of her. Two years previously, her parents had died in a terrible car crash and the brothers had taken over the business and the family. My mother was now employee and homekeeper. Their home was in conflict from the start. Gio believed in self-protection. You looked after you and yours first and you never considered others, however tragic their plight. Tonino said different. You helped yourself but also others. It was the Lord's command. Soon, he would leave the shop and become a teacher. He would also set up a local charity and devote much of his spare time to it. Gio was not impressed by his brother's generosity. When Tonino died unexpectedly of a heart attack, he would bitterly say, 'See where living for others gets you?'

Whilst the brothers quarrelled over their differences, my mother woke early, prepared the food, opened the shop, cleaned it, served people, went upstairs, cooked, ironed and cleaned whilst her brothers took their daily siesta. Then she'd open the shop again, clean, work hard and find herself exhausted by sundown.

And then she met him and life was never the same.

You never knew that such beauty could exist in your world, did you, Papa? It was 1949 and you hadn't travelled. No one had really. The world was huge in those days, impossible to know. So on that fateful day in the Piazza Tasso, when you saw my mother you had to follow her and you had to possess her. And why not? She liked you, my mother. Unlike other Sorrento women, who would have laughed at your entreaties, my mother got interested in you. Do you know why? Because she hadn't seen your like either. You were tall and gentle and polite and cheerful and with your hair swept back and your army captain's uniform pressed – you looked grand, so grand. Striking, that's what you were. But you were something else, as well. You were the key for my mother, the way out. Isn't that true, Mama? My father was the key to escape the life that lay before you, the life that gave you a tiredness no one should know at your young age. That's what Father was, what he really was.

So you smiled and you listened to him and you went on walks and one night, when the stars didn't appear for some reason above the deep bay of Napoli, you finally let his lips circle yours and let his tongue slip inside your mouth and you lost yourself in the moment. For moments such as these were absolutely new to you, fresh and so exciting. He spoke of life in England, he spoke of escape – and the more you fell into his rhythm, his way of talking, his life, the more it made sense. You went on hidden dates with him, for you knew your brothers would disapprove but you couldn't stop yourself until finally you woke one day and you knew your destiny lay with him, the Englishman who had never seen such beauty before.

One fine day you bade goodbye to your resentful brothers and you boarded that huge ship that rolled upon the blue waters. You stood on the deck and you looked back at the pier and you saw your old life standing there, waving goodbye. Goodbye to Sorrento and its sweet smell, borne upon its cobbled streets. Goodbye to Vesuvio and the fishing boats that circle it so respectfully. Goodbye to exhaustion, made worse by the summer heat. Goodbye to the magic of her town. Goodbye to the brothers, sullen and angry but entwined by blood. Goodbye to Sorrento's eternal procession. And goodbye to the basket and the rope. You placed your hand in my father's and made a wish upon your love.

South Africa for the honeymoon, Surrey for the home. I see my mother standing in a yard, struggling to place clothes upon the line in her back yard. It is a cold and unlovely day. To the right and left of her, neighbours talk to each other, their words flying above her head like angry birds. 'Don't like Italians, me,' one of them sniffs, 'not after the war.' My mother hears the words but only understands the tone. She can't speak English, so she retreats inside. She's three months pregnant now with Nina, my sister.

The newly-weds live on food rations. Sometimes she wastes their meals because she doesn't know how to cook this food properly. She misses Sorrento badly but she won't say anything. She has pride, she has belief. She is married and she will stay here, despite all these unlovely days, which come one after the other, unrelenting and so grey. She will not give up on love or her husband, even though since the pregnancy she feels her husband retreating. Confusion. It is not like him to be this way.

In the beginning, in the first flush of their love, he found her shortcomings amusing.

'Don't worry, love, for love will feed us,' he says when her cooking of English food lets her down. He goes and stands behind her at the oven, kisses her head, buries his lips in her dark, wavy hair, puts his arm around her waist and thinks, what a beautiful woman I have caught.

At the weekend, they would go for drives in the country where he set about improving her English. They had fun doing it. 'Monday, Tuesday, Wednesday, Friday,' she would giggle. They smoked cigarettes together and smiled at each other. They ate picnics and kissed upon grey woollen blankets.

But in the week he works as an electrical engineer and during the days the laughter stops and so does the talking and she is left alone with people who 'don't talk to Italians.'

She gets bored and then she gets frightened because she lives in the knowledge that the people round here don't like her. But why? What had she ever done to them? This was not her fault.

He senses her misgivings and gets to thinking. One day he returns with a television. At first she is fascinated but the words are spoken fast and within minutes of turning on the machine she is not sure what she is watching. The English language defeats her. She loses interest in the black-and-white pictures. Her lack of joy at the thing he has specially bought her annoys him. Badly.

Doubt bubbles up from the back of his mind and it clouds his feelings. He thought he would love her forever. Look at her, with her dancing eyes and rich hair. How could you not be swayed by such beauty? Now he knows. The feeling taints forever what was once so pure and unshakeable and so strong in the Piazza Tasso.

His love starts to peel away like old wallpaper. Her looks, her ways of doing things are not doing what they used to do for him. Now there are fewer drives in the country. Now he takes her to pubs, large smoky rooms where people peer at her in her nice coat and her make-up and they make faces at her that she cannot understand.

In the pub, sometimes he leaves her alone, seems to disappear into the blue smoke that surrounds her. She sits alone at the table and smiles but she says nothing. Instead, she thinks of the Piazza Tasso and how nice it would be to buy an ice and walk down the harbour in the hot night, arm in arm with the man who's just disappeared. She recalls the tall buildings, the cobbled alleyways, the basket and the rope to pull up the fruit, the noise, the shouts, that smell which you only find in Sorrento, the pretty cotton dresses she once wore, the smiles of the shopkeepers, the informality, the formality, and she forgets how tired she was back then and the eighteen-hour days she worked, and she sips on her gin and tonic and she smiles at the people who look at her.

Then Nina arrives and diverts them from their crisis. They bind together over their daughter. They have a shared purpose now. They have something in common. So much so that a year later Frankie arrives. The house is further filled with baby clothes and baby food and cries that come at all hours of the day and night.

And still the neighbours won't talk to her and still the grey days come one after the other and the cold and the rain never seem to cease.

She longs for the warmth of the sun to bear down from the grey skies and touch the grey buildings and the grey ground and transform them. But when it doesn't and her husband shouts at her to deal with the babies for he has to go to work to pay for all of this, she feels her soul slip further away from her and she doesn't know what to do.

In a panic, she turns away from him and looks to her children, for it is only then that she is allowed a glimpse of God, a precious thing in this country of unlovely days. But they are children who shout and scream and demand everything. They exhaust her. She has no respite from their claims on her. Sometimes it is all she can do to lie on a sofa and let them play outside together.

When he gets home, the electrical engineer, the husband who rescued her from drudgery in the sun, he curses her laziness. The food is not ready and love no longer beats hunger. Her nerves fray even more. She begins to panic. Everything she gambled upon rested on one certainty – the love of her man. For without him she is nothing. She is an Italian woman living in a small-minded cold town in Surrey. Her family are a million miles away and she does not have the means to reach either them or her husband. All she has is a man who fades from her day after day. That's when my mother realises she has been tricked and that's when the first breakdown comes.

Love betrayed my mother. It said, follow me and I will rescue you. My mama said yes and love laughed out loud, picked her up and then smashed her like a china doll against a stone floor. Love hated my mother. It left her staring at the sky, her soul doused, her spirit silent forever. For years, I hated love.

The first Social Services report that is to be found in my file reports that my mother first came to the attention of the authorities when she was spotted walking the streets of Redhill with her two daughters, muttering about killing herself. The authorities' response was to place her in a psychiatric hospital in Banstead, Surrey. My two sisters were temporarily put into care. The report curtly announces that the father, an electrical engineer, visits the children, 'although infrequently.'

My mother recovers quickly and the family is reunited but it is just a respite. Pretty soon she is back in hospital and she is pregnant. Five days before I am born the hospital realise her condition. My mother hasn't said a word to them yet about her impending third child. Two days after my birth I am taken away from her by the Unknown Nurse, the one I always think about when my mind turns to that fateful night.

Four

The Art of Gracious Living

Redhill, Surrey, 1958

The car drives me to a large house in Woking. Then it returns to Redhill hospital to wait for my mother who is due to return to the hospital that cures minds. She is on drugs now and will be till her dying day. She has been placed in a small ward in the grounds and there is no one to rescue her. She is alone, totally alone.

So she takes her pills and at seven every night she goes to bed. She talks to no one. Her English is not good and what's the point? All she knows is this. She will never, ever sign the forms they put in front of her, the ones that allow these strange people to take away her children. Her children will always be hers. Others may look after them, they may feed them and they may clothe them. But they belong to her. They are her angels. She will not forsake them. In their faces she sees the only light that means anything to her and she will not put out that light for anything or anyone. If she does, she will die for she will have nothing else to live for.

I was placed in a nursery that cared for orphans. I retain few memories from this period, but there is one I will carry forever. I was three years old. It was night-time. I was awake in my cot. The dormitory was silent, the curtains were drawn. I was staring upwards, waiting for sleep. In a flash, I suddenly found myself looking down from the ceiling.

I had no idea what force propelled me there or why. Even so, I was calm. I was not at all scared that I had been entirely liberated from my body. I simply remained aware that I was experiencing something out of the ordinary. I looked down at myself in the cot and then just as quickly, and just as magically, I was that boy again. That was it. I had come back inside myself. I stared at the ceiling for a few minutes and then my eyes betrayed me and I rolled over into sleep. Little did I know I had just experienced the tenor of my life – the one who stays on the outside, looking in.

Naturally, no other memories from this period at the nursery are as striking. I can recall painting lessons, I recall disliking milk and biscuits before going to bed and, for some reason, I recall a brightly coloured stripy T-shirt that I always seemed to wear.

The last thing I remember from the nursery is sitting on the floor playing with a tank one sunny day and a shadow suddenly falling in front of me. I looked up and there she stood, smiling. My new mother, Mrs K. Beside her stood the gentle lady who gave us our meals and tucked us up in bed, and she said if I was really good and I wasn't naughty, then maybe, just maybe, I could go and live with Mrs K. And wouldn't that be nice? To be honest, I really had no idea whether it would be nice or not so I said nothing. I just looked at Mrs K., who smiled at me again and then she put out her hand. I took it.

She wore a long, dark tartan skirt and her brown handbag was clasped tightly in the crook of her elbow. She had long thin fingers and I noted the small wedding ring which, as I would later find out, was as pale as the marriage it represented. Her eyes were light brown, her cheeks slightly sunken, and cruelty lived and breathed beneath the skin of her face. I swear on some occasions I could almost reach out and touch it as it passed through her eyes.

The first job my new mother undertook was to change my identity. My real mother had christened me Paolo Pietro Alberto Hewitt. My second mother didn't like that; she didn't like that at all.

'Your name is Paul now,' she told me smartly, 'not Paolo or Paulo but Paul. You're English. Your name is Paul in English.' We were standing in a room in her house that contained a brown oak table, a small TV, a table with chairs and two armchairs. This is where I would eat and be allowed to watch the occasional evening television programme.

There was a sitting room out to the left of the hall but it never seemed to be used. It just stood there, silent. It was a room that intrigued me; a room I never entered. I often imagined it filled with presents, toys wrapped in boxes and silver paper and decorations; a room which was always Christmas. Which is why I never opened the door and looked in – I knew it was bare.

I spent most of my time in the kitchen area with my new mother. 'Now go outside and play,' Mrs K. told me, 'and you mustn't come back in until I tell you. You'll be a naughty boy if you do. If I see you inside here before I tell you to come in I'll be very annoyed.'

She said it with such firmness that at first it surprised me. She had been calm previously. Now her voice had frightened me a little. I told her I would be good and I wandered out onto the patio.

Directly in front of me stood a hedge and to the left lay a small garden surrounded on all sides by flowers. It was a grey afternoon that hung upon this Friday. I stood motionless, not knowing what to do. In truth, when I was alone I didn't know how to play and what's more I had nothing and no one to play with.

Then I saw a small ball lying on the grass and I gratefully walked towards it. Suddenly, a flurry of barking sprang up from behind me. The noise caught me totally by surprise. I felt as if I had been caught doing something terrible. I turned quickly. A small boxer dog stood about five feet away, angrily barking at me. He rolled his body and I saw a block of muscle ripple threateningly. Panic suffused my whole body. I ran. I ran into the garden and the dog came bounding after me, its barking made even more incessant by my running. I was too young to know its nature, had no idea it was being playful. Alarmed, I began to run in circles. Ring a ring of roses, a boy full of fear. The dog followed, yelping and barking. I dared not stop but I could feel my chest tightening. Then my breath gave out. Panting in terror, I stopped and turned to face my fate. The dog skidded to a halt just a few feet away, confused and angry at my ignorance of his game. He reacted by barking even louder.

The noise triggered off more panic inside me, a horrific liquid, mercury-like, filling my body from my feet to my head. I realised I would have to make it back inside the house. Despite what she had told me, my new mother would understand. She would see how scared I was and she would banish the dog and then comfort me, forgive me my trespasses.

I looked towards the house, got ready to make my move. The dog suddenly barked and made as if to come forward. It was at that moment that I saw, clearly visible in the window, Mrs K. watching me. And not just watching either, but laughing and laughing hard. I now knew for sure that something was not quite right with the new world I found myself in.

In my files, it states that Mrs K. is fond of me but does not want to become a foster parent (temporary guardian without full parental rights) unless it will be possible to fully adopt at some point in the future. The social worker then notes, the 'air of apparent strain' about Mr and Mrs K. and believes they are trying hard to appear 'relaxed.' Their main concern is that my mother's illness is not of a kind likely to recur in me. They will monitor the situation. The social worker understands just how ambitious their educational plans are for me and is sympathetic to their desires.

After just two day visits it was decided that I too should become a K. My bag was packed and I was taken to live in the house with the strange sitting room and the angry dog. One of the first things Mrs K. did was to organise my day.

Breakfast over, it would be time to teach me how to read. Every morning we sat at that brown oak table with books amassed in front of us and she, with those long bony fingers, guided me through to literacy. As words magically opened up to me, the pleasure of reading gripped me hard. I learnt quickly, smoothly. And, naturally, it didn't escape my attention that my growing desire to devour the printed page greatly pleased Mrs K. During these morning lessons, she was so calm, so encouraging, so like a mother should be. I didn't know her plans then.

By now I had been introduced to her husband, Bill, who I had heard about but had never seen on my day visits. Bill, a small, compact man, travelled every day to London to work in an office – the civil service, I later found out – and he fascinated me because his hair was totally white and the tops of some of his fingers were yellow. I had never seen hair that colour or such stained hands. For some reason I thought his nicotine stains came through the endless pots of tea he made his wife.

Bill didn't seem to be around much, although it was he who told me one day that I had a sister. Her name was Elizabeth but she was boarding at a ballet school in Camberley named Elmhurst. Come the holidays she would return and I would meet her. She was four years older than me.

I took in this information and smiled weakly, thinking that this was the right response. Then I returned to my book and he went out to the garden and watered the flowers.

Again, I was out in the garden. Again, I was alone. This is how I spent my afternoons: wandering around the garden, wondering what to do. The dog stayed inside the house. We were friends now, Scottie and I, but Mrs K. wouldn't let me play with him. 'You'll get too dirty,' she explained.

Today, as I listlessly circled the garden, I was hoping against hope that Mrs K. would not be watching me. I was scared because the night before, as I stood naked in shallow lukewarm bath water, she had quizzed me. She had approached with a towel and casually asked, 'Did you enjoy yourself in the garden today?'

'Yes.' It was a lie and I clearly remember it because it was the first time I discovered how lying when you're naked makes your deceit seem that much weaker. My face unavoidably blushed. 'Yes, I did enjoy myself.'

The tone of her voice darkened a little. 'Well, it didn't look like it to me,' she brusquely remarked, wrapping the towel around my small body. She started her rubbing and I had to admit she was right. I had spent a lot of my time that day kneeling down and staring at the flowers, pretending to be interested in their form and colour. I didn't know what else to do. There was nothing and no one to play with. Now she was making me feel like it was my fault.

'Don't you know how to play?' It was a question pitched at an innocent level but underwritten by an accusatory manner. I knew straight away that to answer in the negative would lead to instant trouble.

'Yes.'

'You're not so stupid that you don't know how to play, *are you?*' The emphasis was strongly put on the 'are you?' and I instantly knew that in her eyes stupidity was the worst crime imaginable.

'No. I'm not.' I could hardly look her in the face.

'Good,' she said, sternly. And she carried on rubbing, but just a little bit harder.

Now, once again banished to the garden, on this lifeless day, I kept a careful eye out for her. I wanted to show her I knew how to enjoy myself. I wanted to please her. I circled the garden, imagining ways of playing if she should suddenly appear at the window. But that day she never materialised until it was time to come in for dinner. For the next three days the same routine occurred. I would wake, breakfast and read and write in the morning. Then lunch, then go outside. I would wander round the garden, look up and seeing the window frame empty I would carry on. Again. I would look up. Nothing. The frame was clear.

And then one afternoon I looked up and there she was. Staring. I felt my cheeks flush. Instantly, I turned my back on her as my mind furiously started conjuring up ways of showing her that I was having a great time. That I was smart. That I knew how to play. I started to run. I ran to the end of the garden, stretched out my arms and then turned, making engine noises with my tongue. Look, I am an aeroplane. That's what little boys like, isn't it, being aeroplanes? I ran forward, conscious of her presence but halfway up the garden I tripped over myself and I crashed to the ground. I was hurt. My knee was grazed and my forehead was stinging but that was nothing to the shame I could feel setting my entire body on fire. I stayed still, face-down in the keen-smelling grass, not knowing what I should do. When I could finally bear to look up my new mother had disappeared. She was not at the window. I spent the rest of the day uneasy about what the night might bring but at tea she never mentioned the incident – never shouted at me for getting my jumper dirty or my knee bloodied; for being so stupid as to trip myself up. I kept waiting for her to explode. But she never did. And it drove me mad.

I hated having to think up new ways of playing. I tried once to be a fireman but holding an imaginary hose that doused invisible burning houses and hospitals felt so stupid. I went back to being a soldier, holding a pretend gun and shooting at invisible enemies. But that too embarrassed me. I was no good at being a playful child, no good at pretending to be one, either. Already, life had turned me serious. All I liked was reading in the morning. That was it. When the book slammed shut for the day, so did my life.

Then Elizabeth arrived. She was nothing like I imagined her. I had imagined meeting a graceful child ballerina, elegant in body, charming in nature. The girl who appeared in front of me defied all my expectations. Elizabeth wore huge glasses and was strikingly overweight. I could not for the life of me imagine her in a ballerina's dress. I was puzzled but, of course, said nothing.

On her first night home, just as we were sitting down to eat, Mrs K. told Elizabeth to bring her school report to the table.

'I'm sure it's absolutely wonderful,' she said.

Elizabeth returned to the table, handed over a small grey book with a crest on its front and then sat with her head bowed whilst my new mother scanned its contents. When she finished, Mrs K. placed the report softly on the table. She took a breath and then she reached over, grabbed a handful of Elizabeth's hair and violently jerked herself and her daughter to their feet. Both their chairs howled in sharp anguish, scraping against the stone floor.

'This is disgraceful!' she screamed. 'All the money we pay for you to attend the best school and you come home with this?' she yelled. 'Last in everything. What do you mean by this? Tell me! Are you really as stupid as you look, you fat, horrible girl?'

I kept my head down, hardly dared to look at my plate. I heard Mrs K.'s hand slap Elizabeth's head. Several times. And when Elizabeth cried I looked up and saw Mrs K. turn to her husband, who had remained totally silent throughout it all, his face, like mine, averted from the scene, and scream: 'Bill, I never want to see this girl again.' Then she stormed out of the room.

Elizabeth stood there sobbing, her large shoulders heaving.

Bill quickly said, 'Sit down, Elizabeth.' He tried to say it firmly but his inaction at his wife's violence had already betrayed his essential character: weak. I looked at him and he looked away.

Two days later, Elizabeth took me into the garden, pulled my hair hard, pinched my arm and told me I was a nasty, horrible, fat boy and that one day she would kill me. In the meantime, I was to obey her every command. I was scared but the next day, to my relief, she went back to ballet school and a day later she had totally vanished from my mind. This left me striving to become the brightest boy in the whole wide world. All for Mrs K., my brand new mother.

Two women now came into my life. Grandmothers – mothers of Bill and Mrs K., both were kind souls, surprisingly so in the case of Mrs K.'s mother. One time, Bill's mother took me to the cinema to see the film *Dr. Who and the Daleks.* After watching the show on the small black-and-white TV in the kitchen, the film totally overwhelmed me. What an experience. You sat in this vast semi-lit room, staring at this strange white screen, occasionally glancing round at others, some looking on in similar bewilderment, and then the lights dimmed and suddenly a torrent of sound and colour assaulted you. It picked you up and put you in another dimension. I was transfixed, overwhelmed, until finally I found my balance and started to concentrate on the film. I soon picked up its rhythm but I was confused. I couldn't see how Dr. Who, with his limited human powers, could ever defeat the Daleks. They were like Mrs K.: unbeatable. But somewhere along the line I missed something and in the twist of a minute the good Doctor was suddenly on top, and in a pulsating ending the Daleks were destroyed and the house lights were on and my initial fears had turned to complete exhilaration.

I remember thinking two things as we walked home from the cinema. Already I knew that such a wondrous experience could never have been given to me by my Mrs K. The second was that I now hoped that the gentle woman who had opened up this new world for me would turn to me, here, right here on the street, and say, 'Right, Paul, I can see you're worried, unhappy. You come and live with me now.'

But she never did and, really, if I'm honest, I knew she wouldn't.

Mrs K. took me to the nearest Catholic church and I became an altar boy. Every Sunday I held the big candle at mass. It was my big moment. One day Father Tucker, a kindly, portly Irishman with black hair, told me that I had a guardian angel, sent by God to look out for me. I told Mrs K. this story. She confirmed it, and added that this angel was checking on me every day and every minute and that if I was a bad boy it would count against me if I ever went to Heaven.

I thought about this and then wondered if it was a he or a she. And then I thought that if it was with me at all times, was it with me when I went to the toilet? Or did he or she disappear when I entered and sat on the seat? I figured in the end that when I took down my shorts my guardian angel looked away, especially if it was a she.

We moved to a big house in Bagshot, Surrey, and suddenly there was a sense of newness about my life. The Beatles were on the radio singing, 'She loves you, yeah, yeah, yeah,' and I had fresh surroundings to explore. Bill had been promoted at work, hence the grander location. The new house, with its white walls and driveway and front garden, was huge; it was entered through a door at the right-hand side of the building. You walked into the hallway and to your right was a set of stairs that led up to a bathroom and four bedrooms, mine being the smallest. When you came downstairs to the hall, if you turned back on yourself, on the left was a room that, again, was rarely used but was dominated by a long dining table. This was only to be used for special meals.

'You'll have your birthday parties here, Paul,' she told me. I never did.

Next to that room was a study and as you walked past the study you came to a couple of steps leading up to a large sitting room. In here there was a television and a telephone although the phone never seemed to ring. I don't think phones did in the '60s.

To the right of this room was a large kitchen divided in two by a doorway, but with no door. In the first half of this space meals were prepared, washing-up duties undertaken. Through its window you looked out onto the large back garden where a roofless brick barn stood. In the second half of the kitchen, where we ate the majority of our meals, there was a stone floor and a table with four chairs. A radio was placed on the shelf opposite the table and that's how I first heard The Beatles. It was a Sunday morning and I was being sent horse riding. I was eating cornflakes when this sound erupted from the radio. It had energy and force and this chorus that just latched itself onto my brain. 'She loves you, yeah, yeah, yeah, she loves you...'

Invigorated, I left the house alone. The morning air was fresh and new and as I tramped down wet country paths, the song came to my mind again. As it did it triggered something inside me and the very next second I was suffused by an ecstasy I had never known before. The song danced in my head, a magnificent warmth filled me. Joyfully, I just kept singing the song over and over to myself as I stamped through the leaves and the wet grass. 'She loves you, yeah, yeah, yeah, She loves you, yeah, yeah, yeah.' I felt truly invincible.

Then I was at the stables and they put me on the horse and I fell off it and I never went back there again. But that was the day music came into my life and revealed its power to me. I've never forgotten. It is why I have spent my life searching for that first feeling, again and again.

Music, like books and films before, had shown me a way out of my reality, a reality that was turning increasingly nasty thanks to Mrs K.'s unpredictable behaviour. Some days I could do nothing right and she would scream at me. Other days, she wouldn't say a word and I would have to tiptoe around her like you would a sleeping poisonous snake.

I developed bad eczema on the inside of my arms. I heard the doctor say you caught it through worry. Mrs K. said, 'Oh, he's probably worrying about his pocket money,' and they laughed together and he left the house carrying his small bag of magic. I was given a cream to soothe my rash but at night, in my sleep, I would scratch at the irritation with such vigour that I would wake with bleeding sores. Mrs K.'s solution was simple. At night, I would get into bed and she would order me to show her my wrists. She would then wrap bandages around them. Firmly handcuffed, I would then lie down and try and sleep.

Yet when I awoke I would have broken free of the bandages and my arms would be bleeding. Mrs K. would enter the room to wake me and the sight would infuriate her. I would receive a hard slap on the legs. 'You silly boy, can't you even sleep properly?' One morning I awoke and to my horror discovered that I had now soaked the sheets with urine and that the bandages were again loose.

For that I was slapped hard on both legs and bottom. I started crying and the sound drove her to even further extremes. 'Stop that crying, you disgusting boy, stop it.'

Then I would dress and come down to eat breakfast under her stern gaze.

The only treat I recall from my time with Mrs K. occurred when The Beatles played *Sunday Night at the London Palladium* and I was unexpectedly allowed to stay up past my bedtime to watch them. I was five years old and so thrilled. Like so many of us at that time, I was Beatle mad. Their songs brought wonderment into my life. Every time I heard them, I thrilled at being able to get so close to real magic.

Of course, I was not allowed to buy anything relating to them. That was beneath me, Mrs K. informed me. But I believe that, like all of the country at the time, she was secretly fascinated by their ability to affect people so wildly. Mrs K. would never admit to such vulgar thoughts; she was far too uptight. But that night, 22 October 1963, an exception was being made. That night I could watch The Beatles. Not just listen to them. But watch them. On TV. Incredible. I'd never experienced such a treat before. I felt bubbles stir in my stomach when I heard the news.

After another tense supper had finished, I went into the sitting room and sat on the sofa, with Mrs K. to the left of me. Inside my body, in its very pit, I felt excitement surge and then dash itself against the very real worry that at any moment now she would snap out of her benevolent mood and sharply order me to bed. It wouldn't have surprised me. It was exactly the kind of punishment that she loved using: an offer with one hand, smack around the head with the other.

As I struggled to banish such thoughts from my mind, Mrs K. stood, went over and flicked on the small black-and-white television set that sat in isolation in the left-hand corner of the room. She sat down beside me and as she did so the show began. I saw a large curtain open and to my absolute astonishment the four of them suddenly appeared holding instruments, wearing their usual dark suits – playing, singing, smiling, laughing, absolutely loving life and themselves.

I was caught blind. I hadn't expected to see them so early but before I could work out what was happening, the curtain cruelly closed. They were gone. Vanished. I looked at the small screen in absolute bewilderment. 'It's all right,' Bill said gently, sitting alone on a chair on the other side of the room, 'they're coming back at the end of the show.' A shot of fear now zinged through me. I knew this would be in an hour's time and I hadn't expected to be allowed to stay up that late. I thought the four of them would be on during the show, not at the end, not at the finale. The delay in their appearance now meant that Mrs K. had every excuse to send me upstairs. All she had to do was turn to me, say, 'Paul, they're on too late, go to bed.'

I sat in a tense silence as act after meaningless act appeared on the screen, did their thing and then left. None of them made any impression on me whatsoever. I was watching the TV but seeing nothing. I was just keeping my gaze steady and desperately ignoring Mrs K.

Then, after a thousand prayers to my guardian angel, The Beatles finally returned and, as always when they entered my life, I forgot everything, even the malevolent presence who still sat quietly beside me, not moving, not stirring. The Beatles thrilled me that night, even more so when one of the songs they announced was mine. It was 'She Loves You.' I was mesmerised. That band entered me, took over again and filled me with the magic I felt on that exhilarating Sunday morning.

Again, they had effortlessly created that special world I could climb inside and live in.

Then it was over and I was climbing the stairs to my bed in my pyjamas and dressing gown. I was five years old and my name was Paul K. Or Paolo. Or Paulo. I wasn't sure. But really I was Paul McCartney because I had hair like his. The world was somehow different that night and I felt good. I did. For that night, I felt good. Still I remember it. Yeah, yeah, yeah.

I liked Father Tucker because he was solid, gentle, his moods never varying. His whole demeanour was calm, unflappable, and he was the second person I wanted to be. I looked up at him in both senses of the word and I envied him. His life seemed so ordered, so right and, above all, gentle. And then one day he shocked me.

Father Tucker told me at catechism class that we were born in sin. We were not, as I had thought, innocent babies who dirtied our souls on earth. That was not the story. No. Somehow, and I couldn't figure out how, we were already soiled when we were born. I couldn't believe it. How could a baby sin? How? It was impossible. I thought about this shocking revelation in the bath that night and it led me to wonder exactly where my soul was located. I knew the location of my heart and my stomach and my chest but no one had yet told me where my soul was.

I looked down and soon decided that my soul must be at the centre of my body and that my belly button was its entry point. My mind whirred backwards and turned to the sins I had committed that day. I mentally counted them up. They came to three. Pretending not to hear Mrs K. calling me when I was in the garden; wishing her dead; and wanting to steal sweets when I walked past a shop that afternoon. I idly peeked inside my belly button and gasped. Clearly visible were four lines of dirt. It was obvious what they were. My three sins plus the original sin we were all born with.

With a terrible shudder I now realised that every time I committed a sin a black mark appeared on my belly button. Worse, if I ever lied to a priest about my sins, well, no wonder it was a grave, stupid offence because all he would have to do was lift up my shirt and count the lines. I then realised that my guardian angel must have been watching me in the very act of this discovery so I quickly got out of the bath, hastily dressed for bed and then, handcuffed as usual by Mrs K., tried to pull the blankets over my head and my sins, praying for sleep and for the darkness.

Time's love always turns to hate. As children, time comes and envelopes us, lingers by our side, refusing to leave. When our souls are young, time is our most ardent admirer. Yet children push it away. They want so badly to hurry up the world. Time shakes its head at our folly because it knows what we do not; that in youth, time must take its time.

So time clicks by slowly, so slowly in fact that we take our eye off it until one day we're adults and suddenly time is a fast car, and now it races away, quickly, sharply, never failing to taunt us with its pace, mocking us as we try to grasp and hold onto it. It's shocking. Time was once our friend and now time is our enemy.

Sometimes we would drive down to Mrs K.'s mother's in Bognor. Bill drove a four-seater green Humber car. It had brown leather seats and every time I climbed inside the smell of the leather would disgust me and make me gag. I would feel sick gather in my stomach. That was when Mrs K. would turn to me and say, 'Paul, if you're sick there will be no pocket money when we get to Grandmother's.'

I nodded and tried ignoring my stomach's increasing turbulence. But it was no good and I knew it. Ten minutes down the road I started retching. Bill hastily pulled over and I jumped out, let it all out in spasms that seemed to last forever. No one came to help or comfort me.

I returned to the car and we drove off. There was silence. Just the hum of the motor. Then, casually, as she stared ahead at the road, Mrs K. announced, 'That's no pocket money for two weeks. You didn't even try, you stupid boy.' I stared out of the window, felt resentment scour my cheeks.

At her mother's large dark house, I sat in silence. I didn't move, didn't say a word. I just answered questions and spoke when I was spoken to. That was what she expected. Eventually, after asking to be excused, I went to the toilet and on the way back I was surprised by Joss, my gran's husband. Joss was a distant figure to me. He never came to our house, never visited as his wife did. So I was fascinated when he motioned me into an empty room and then put half a crown in my hand. He slipped it in so quick I wasn't sure for a second what he had given me. Then I realised and I happily put the large silver coin in my pocket and we walked back together into the room. It was our secret, mine and Joss's. On the journey home, as was my habit, I stared out at the black countryside. I saw single bare trees that stood hard in cold, bare fields. I studied their angular, peculiar shapes, felt their latent menace. Deep forests suddenly appeared. My gaze turned upwards and I studied the tops of the trees swaying with a terrifying abandon in the wind, propelled, I believed, by some kind of demonic force. I shuddered and my eyes stared into the thick forest itself and I felt fear slash me inside. I was so frightened by the shape of the forest, its immense depth and what it contained. I imagined being sucked into that black hole and I shivered inside.

The feeling reminds me of dreams I have recently been experiencing. Twice I am walking in a country lane when a huge force surprises me from behind and grips me, lifts me off my feet and pushes me towards what I know is a terrible fate and I have to wake myself up before I reach this hazardous destination.

Suddenly, Mrs K.'s sharp voice broke my dark dreamings. 'Paul, give me the money Grandfather Joss gave you.'

In a stunned manner, I slid my hand into my pocket and pulled out the huge coin. I handed it over. It was incredible. We were alone when Joss gave me the big coin that my tiny hands could hardly cover, yet somehow she knew about his gift. How? Was there anything that could escape her evil attentions? Anything?

I sat back and looked at the blacked-out fields that we passed and realised that her hold over me was now truly absolute. Her grip was all-encompassing. A forest passed us by but even the black woods could not stir my fear like this woman just had. I felt my soul recoil like a snake, slowly wrapping itself around a dark tree. A month later Grandfather Joss died.

And then we moved to London. It was strange but it wasn't. One day we were in this nice Bagshot house and then we were in a cramped flat in Shepherd's Bush. Elizabeth now joined us. Her ballet career was over. It was 1965 – of that I can be sure. Winston Churchill's funeral was on the TV and a gloom seemed to seep through the screen as the solemn march of his death took forever to unwind in front of us. Mrs K. made us watch it all the way through. Hour after hour of it. In absolute silence. It was as if we were to blame for his passing.

One morning, when both Bill and Mrs K. had gone out, Elizabeth said, 'I've got something to show you.' She went over to the mantelpiece and picked up the small radio. She sat down and switched the dial. Suddenly this twisting guitar riff came blasting out into the room. This sound was so fresh, so exciting.

'It's a new station,' she told me above the noise, 'it's a pop station. It only plays pop music.' I sat and listened to the song playing. 'It's The Beatles,' she said. "You like them, don't you? The song is called "Ticket To Ride".'

Her glasses looked big and she was still very overweight but I could sense she was reaching out to me. Which is why I think of her most times that song is played. Then we heard the door go and she hurriedly turned off the radio and we picked up books and pretended we were reading.

Two weeks later she was gone for good. 'She isn't living here any more,' Mrs K. brusquely told me. I don't know where she went but I wished she was around to reach out some more to me. I think she could have been a lot of fun. Instead, just as Elizabeth had suspected, her days had been numbered and I had been brought in to replace her.

I was good at reading and terrible at most other subjects, yet I wanted so badly to succeed at school, wanted so badly to please Mrs K. I had been placed in a local comprehensive school deep in Shepherd's Bush. One afternoon the art teacher told us we were to create a drawing which we would then give to our parents as a surprise. It could be of anything we liked. She told us to begin. I looked at the white paper in front of me and thought that if I failed in this mission my teacher would ring Mrs K. and tell her. My penchant for taking everything too seriously was now apparent. Worried, I began thinking of what to draw but, as usual, my imagination, like a lot inside me, was frozen. I had no idea what to draw.

By the end of the class I had made a few lines on a large piece of white paper and little else. I had nothing to take home. It was then that I noticed one of my classmates talking to the art teacher. He had left his drawing on his desk. Without even thinking about it, I simply walked over, picked it up, rolled it under my arm and left the room. It was the first time I had ever stolen anything.

I went home and proudly said to Mrs K., 'I've done this drawing for you.'

She unrolled the paper, studied it for three seconds and then her right hand came flying round and smacked me right across the head. She pushed me backwards into my bedroom.

'Go to bed right now,' she screamed, 'and in the morning you can give it back to the poor boy you stole it from.' Then she turned sharply on her heel and slammed the door, leaving me in the darkness with a drawing that I hated, that I wished so badly I had never taken home. Especially when I finally saw what Mrs K. had spotted, written in small letters in the bottom right-hand corner of the picture. It was the boy's name and our class number emblazoned in yellow crayon.

Around this time, according to my files, Mrs K. tells the Social Services that she and Bill want to adopt another child. They give them a list. They do not mind about the child's sex but he or she must be between the ages of three and four, can be foreign including Indian, central European and Scandinavian but must not be Negro. They prefer the child to be Church of England, not a bed-wetter and not prone to travel sickness. The child must also be intelligent and tolerably good-looking. In a bemused tone, the social worker tells Mrs K. that it would be practically impossible to find such a child. Mrs K. brushes her off, says airily, fine, leave it for a few months. If you have nothing suitable by then, we will look elsewhere.

In the summer of 1966, I saw Mods revving their scooters on Brighton sea front and I felt Mrs K.'s disgust at their freedom. As we walked past them I had to look back before I was jerked away. That Mod summer, I also felt the first tinges of love but it was not for any girl or a glorious lifestyle. It was for the beautiful game.

On 22 June, I sat in amazement and watched England beat Germany, saw England become world champions. World champions. It seemed an incredible thing to achieve. I watched the match at Mrs K.'s mother's house and then she allowed me to go out and kick a ball against a wall for hours on end. In doing so, I discovered something new to lose my mind to. The book and the ball would become my closest friends.

I couldn't help noticing the incredibly sharp difference between mother and daughter, between the icy, unpredictable Mrs K. and her mother, this kindly, elegant woman with the curly grey hair and the nice jewellery and the fine clothes; this woman who always smiled and who allowed me to breathe and just be.

I think Mrs K. felt the disparity as well. I think she saw it as a threat. That was why, one Sunday afternoon in front of my grandmother's worried pale eyes, she started a row with me. My knees were dirty. Bad boy. Very bad boy. Mrs K. stood up, took me by my collar and pushed me into a cupboard that was built under the stairs. She did so for no reason other than that my knees were dirty. I was to stay there until she said I could come out. I nodded and she closed the door.

I sat there and slowly my eyes adjusted to the light. I sat still, knowing then that she had forced me into this dark corner as a show of force towards her own mother. She was also telling me something: kill any dreams of being rescued by your kindly grandmother. I won't allow that to happen.

In the cupboard I didn't cry, nor was I particularly scared. Instead, I felt I had been ordained for such cruelty, like a priest who feels his calling. It was a strange sensation. I also knew that this cruelty was going to escalate. Being locked in a cupboard was the start. Everything that had gone before was just a rehearsal. This was where the real stuff began. I shivered against the wall and waited for the door to open.

A social worker comes to my rescue. Writing after a visit to my home, she notes that on her arrival I am brusquely ordered to take a walk by my foster mother and I fetch my coat, gloves and scarf in 'a very self-possessed way.' After I leave, Mrs K. then shows the social worker a letter from a doctor that describes in detail my mother's illness and states that as far as she is concerned I am now in the early stages of the same disease. Unlike Elizabeth, who might have had a low IQ, I am completely impractical. I keep dropping things all the time. I can't figure out how things work. My actions are really getting on Mrs K.'s nerves. I irritate her so much and now she has grave, very grave doubts about my mental health.

My social worker hits the alarm bells. She writes that she is 'very concerned about this child in his foster home.' She has made many visits to my home and on every occasion she found me to be too controlled, too rigid for a child of my age. Mrs K.'s emphasis on my education has blinded everyone to what is really happening and that the situation should be viewed 'in a psychiatric light rather than from a purely educational viewpoint.' She writes like a woman determined to rescue me. Then, for some unfathomable reason, she is taken off my case. I am assigned a new social worker. He is male, middle-class and so carelessly stupid. He writes after his first visit that, although the Home I live in has been described as lacking in warmth and that I am too disciplined, he actually finds it refreshing to go into a home where the child is being taught 'the art of gracious living and where the small courtesies of life are of value.'

'Paul,' he breezily concludes, 'appears to be very happy and there are no problems.'

Just my luck to be handed over to such a man.

This occurred in the summer that Mrs K. rented a cottage in Elmer Regis, near the seaside town of Bognor. Come September, I was sent to a local school. I didn't fit in and nor did my closest friend there, Blackie, who suffered that name because of the colour of his skin.

One evening, on the bus home, I stood up, the bus jerked and I fell forward and smacked my head against the iron corner of the seat. I didn't feel too much, didn't realise I had cut my forehead open badly. A girl my age, sitting by, stood up and grabbed me. She said, 'You've really hurt yourself.'

I denied it. So many times. A public fuss was the last thing I wanted. 'No, you have,' she insisted. 'You have. Look.'

She pulled out a small white handkerchief with lace in the corner, dabbed my forehead with it and held it up.

'I'm taking you home,' she said.

When we got there, Mrs K. opened the door, took one look at the situation and transformed herself. She thanked the girl profusely and invited her in. She tended lovingly to my wound. She spoke softly with the girl. She told her that it was my birthday soon and that she really must come to my birthday party. She gave her lemonade and biscuits and said that she would see her at my party. I said nothing. I knew it was a dream even before the girl left. When the girl departed, Mrs K.'s voice changed into her snarl. 'Right, Paul, go to bed now. There's no supper for you, you blundering idiot.'

And then we were back in Bagshot, the white house where the green Humber car which made me sick stood in the garage and the leaves gathered on the lawn – and where Mrs K. now had a lock fitted on the outside of my bedroom door. As I lay in bed, hands bound by bandages, dreading sleep, I would hear that lock snap into place. It was the most ominous noise in my life at that time.

I would awake in the morning, bandages hanging from my wrists, the crooks of my arms sore and bleeding, sheets stained by urine. And the terror in my heart would start pumping again.

I found solace in the church. I found myself – despite the mass being said in Latin – enjoying the ritual of Sunday altar mornings. I liked the incense which poured out of the swinging chalices. I liked some of the hymns that were sung and the sound of massed voices. I loved the fact that Mrs K. was a Protestant and didn't attend mass. I loved being involved in this ceremony. It gave me a kind of importance even if all I did was hold a massive candle at the side of the altar.

They sent me another social worker, Mr Rowland. He was a tall, diffident man and, like Bill, his hair was a shocking white. During his occasional visits, I would sit at the kitchen table with my head bowed, my eyes trained downwards, studying the occasional grey fleck that disrupted the dark stone floor underneath my feet. Once in a while I would look up, take glances at Mr Rowland's head and try to figure out who had the whitest hair, Mr Rowland or Bill. I hoped that my hair would never turn that colour.

Mr Rowland came to tell me that my real mother lived in a hospital and that I had two other sisters, Frankie and Nina. He visited them as well. When he provided this information I fleetingly wondered if they acted in the same disinterested way as I did towards him. They were excited, he said, about having a brother.

Mr Rowland relayed all this in a tone that suggested important news was being imparted and that I should react accordingly. But to me his words meant nothing. My mind was far too occupied with Mrs K., whilst my ability to spontaneously react to the world around me had been forever tempered by the fear of her unpredictable reactions. She cast upon me a dark shadow under which I constantly lived. And when my thoughts were not focused on her, they occasionally turned in a bemused manner to contemplating how I possessed two mothers – one ill, one evil. Set against that puzzle, the discovery of two sisters was neither here nor there.

Mr Rowland usually came in the afternoons and these meetings always ended with him asking me how I was. This was my cue to look up earnestly at him and, barefaced, say that I was fine. He asked more questions. Was there anything I wanted? Was I being fed and looked after all right? Were things okay?

Yeah, yeah, yeah. I mean yes, yes and yes. (Mustn't speak badly now, must I?)

In a way I did want to tell him that I was unhappy, that Mrs K. frightened me, that she'd hit Elizabeth and terrorised me. But I couldn't because, put simply, Mr Rowland did not seem a strong enough man. He was too bland, too unassuming. In a contest against Mrs K. he didn't stand a chance. She would beat him down easily. She would always be triumphant, victorious in her evil. Nothing could stop her. Not even the man whose job it was. So I said nothing. Nothing at all.

He said it was very important that I understood that my true mother, who lay in some distant hospital, had refused to make Mrs K. my official mother. She was still my foster mum and my real mother was my true mother and would remain so until she signed me away on a special piece of paper. Which she never would. I didn't see the point of this information. I didn't see it because quite frankly it didn't stop the terror I lived in.

I was sent to the barber's for my usual short back and sides. I hated this cut but Mrs K. always forced it upon me. The style made my ears stick out, made me feel so foolish as I walked down the road. I imagined everyone passing me and then breaking into a huge smile. In the small hairdresser's I sat in a large chair and the barber began. He was a man of very few words, which was fine by me. As he cut, a hair fell onto my cheek. It was small but it was coarse and my face started itching.

The irritation grew worse. I remained silent. I longed to bring my right arm from under the sheet wrapped around me and brush it away. But I was too scared to tell the barber to stop. I thought he might shout at me. So I determined to keep quiet. I told myself, don't say a word, leave it alone. It was a test for me to keep quiet and bear the irritation. I sat motionless for half an hour and when the silent barber of Bagshot finally motioned to say he was finished, I leapt out of the chair and gratefully rubbed the itch away.

But I had kept quiet. I hadn't said a word. I felt so proud, as if I had just passed a test from God.

'They propose,' says a report on my file about the K.s, 'to go on holiday to Italy this year...the holiday will be expensive but I feel that this is a deserving case...'

My first trip abroad was to Czenatico in Italy, a two-week break. I was sick on the plane and expected a verbal smacking but in public Mrs K. always played the dutiful mother. And as she patted my back and gently explained to others it was my first time on a plane, all the passengers said, 'Ahhh...' I felt sick again. Not only was she the possessor of my soul, she was also a brilliant actress.

Most mornings we went down to the beach where I played in the sand and the sun turned my body brown, so much so that local children and their mothers would approach and talk to me in Italian. I could not speak the language that was mine by birth. I would look at them with real incomprehension and they would walk away cursing me, thinking me rude.

One night, Bill took me out for a walk. We walked through the town in the dark balmy air. Bill smoked a cigarette and neither of us said a word. Then we stopped at a shop window and Bill asked me if there was anything I wanted. I saw a plastic gun and sailor's sword and pointed at it.

'I'd like them,' I said but never thought I'd get them. Then we dropped back into silence and walked away. I think Mrs K. dazed him as much as she did me. I think she filled his mind and made conversation impossible between us. That night was the closest I ever felt to my foster father.

The next evening he handed over the gun and sword.

Most nights in Italy, when we had returned from the beach, Mrs K. would order me to strip. Then she would push me into the shower and, with a small soapy brush, try and scrub away my tan. Bill would look away, pretending all was okay.

'You're English, not Italian,' she would growl, as she attacked my skin with an almost manic strength. 'You're not going home looking like this.' Then she would scrub even harder as if it was my fault that the sun cooked my skin to such a degree. I was glad to come home from the country that I had been denied.

Back in England, one evening after dinner, Mrs K. sat me down, told me the future as she had written it. I would go to a public school soon. There I would learn Latin and the classics. On reaching eleven I would swiftly pass all exams and that would allow me entry into a school such as Harrow or Haileybury. Even Eton was mentioned. After finishing at public school, on it would be to Cambridge or Oxford. I was surprised by her conciliatory tone and I looked up to see that the cruelty that normally coloured her pale, thin cheeks had vanished, and had somehow been replaced by a softer hue.

She continued painting my future with a pronounced tone of kindness, as if she was giving me something really precious and so therefore it was beholden upon me to not let her down. I wouldn't let her down, would I? – Paul? Paul? Would you, Paul?

'No, I won't. I'll do anything to please. Really, I will.'

I was enrolled in a public school called The Manor. On schooldays, I would be woken by Mrs K. She would pull back the sheet and grimace at the loose bandages. She would turn and then slam the bedroom door. I would dress and come downstairs. I would sit quietly at the table and take a silent breakfast. As I ate, Mrs K. would leave the room to prepare herself for the day's activities. It was then that I would go to her handbag on the chest of drawers behind me. I would gently open it, take out her dark-brown leather purse, unclasp it and remove a coin or two, usually pennies, occasionally sixpences. Then I would return to the table and finish breakfast. But my thieving didn't stop there. On the walk down College Lane into the small village that is Bagshot, I would sneak up the garden paths of one of the small houses on my left (a long hedge ran down the right-hand side) and carefully remove the owner's morning paper from the letterbox.

I would hastily put the paper into my satchel and then run back onto the lane, carry on my journey, covered by a cap, a dark raincoat, grey socks and lace-up shoes. On reaching the end of the lane I would cross over the main road and go straight into the village sweet shop. The proprietor, an old bespectacled woman, always sat out the back of the shop. Her absence from the counter was God's morning gift to me. By the time she had roused herself to serve me, my coat pockets would be filled with chocolate bars.

I would then pretend – much to her exasperation – that she didn't have what I wanted and leave to catch my train. There, in a six-seater compartment, I would sit with businessmen who wore suits and bowler hats and carried briefcases and who never said a word. I would settle between them, pull out my stolen newspaper, usually *The Times* or *The Telegraph*, and study it, just like they did. One day, I thought, this will be me, on a train, in a suit, going to London, going to the office. That will make Mrs K. happy.

On arrival at school, the first thing I would do would be to wait for the cloakroom to empty and, with my heart beating faster, I would ransack all the boys' blazers for sweets or coins. Normally, one boy would forget to remove his belongings from his coat. I would then walk into assembly and with the rest of the school say my prayers for the day and promise to be good for the rest of my life.

My form teacher was Mr Snow and my Latin and sports master was Mr Frith. Mr Frith was the quickest dresser I have ever encountered. He would enter his little room to change for a game and within a minute be standing in front of us in shorts and boots and black top, ready to officiate. I thought he had some kind of magic about him. I still do.

At home, at night, we ate in silence. When he finished, Bill would put down his knife and fork and, with his yellow-stained fingers, reach into his pocket and produce a pack of Players cigarettes.

'Oh Bill,' Mrs K. would say, slightly exasperated, 'do you have to smoke?'

'But everyone's finished eating, dear.'

'I know that,' she'd snap, 'I'm not stupid.'

Mrs K. would then tilt her head a certain way and fix him with a cold stare, challenging him, daring him, to light up. Bill was weak, no match for her, and although he would actually challenge her for twenty seconds or so by staring back at her, his resolve had no strength, no conviction. He would put the cigarette into his mouth, the sight of which intensified Mrs K.'s gaze into something even more threatening, but he had no intention of lighting it. He would soon take it out again. As he did, the tension, always that tension whenever she was present, slowly slipped away.

Humiliated, Bill would replace the cigarette in the packet and with a pronounced sigh, stand up and leave the room. Mrs K. would say nothing. She simply kept looking straight at his empty chair, triumphant again. Poor, weak Bill. He was in the same boat as me and she knew it.

Mrs K. would now turn to me. 'Paul, help me wash up and then you can go to the study and complete your homework.'

I'd gather dishes off the wooden table and then stand by her at the sink. She scrubbed each plate with the same vigour that she had attacked my body in Italy. I hated drying up, I hated standing this close to her. It scared me. Inevitably, a plate would slip through my small, nervous hands and smash upon the floor.

'God,' she'd scream, 'you're so clumsy. Get a dustpan and brush up the mess you've made right now. I'm taking this week's pocket money to pay for your stupidity. And don't touch any more plates. Leave them to dry.' After sweeping up the remnants I'd carefully return to the sink where Mrs K. would stand, gazing through a small window out into the black night.

'I don't know what's wrong with you,' she'd snarl. 'I can't even trust you to wipe one single plate. You're so hopeless.' Now, she would only hand me cutlery. I'd take each knife, fork and spoon one by one and pray that it would remain firm in my grasp, not clatter against the floor. I'd look at the clock and tell myself that soon I would be in the study reading Latin books. I had trouble with languages, not my thing at all. But at least there, for one gracious hour, I was alone.

One morning I took the largest amount yet from her purse. I left her with a shilling change from three and sixpence. As soon as I got to school I was taken aside by Mr Snow and informed that Mrs K. had called the school. She'd said I had stolen a lot of money from her purse. She wanted the school to retrieve as much of it as they could. Mr Snow, a thin, tall man with black hair and small blue eyes placed within an angular face, waited for a reaction. I gave him none.

'After class this morning, I want you to stay behind,' he said.

At lunchtime Mr Snow and I sat in the empty classroom. Around me, sitting at their desks, were the ghosts of all my classmates. Some were staring at me. Some were smiling. Others were reading their books.

'I want you to tell me about home,' Mr Snow said. I didn't, couldn't reply.

'Are you happy?' 'Yes.'

'Do you get on well with your parents? Your father?' That was easy. 'Yes.'

'Your mother?' 'Yes, yes.'

'So why are you stealing from her?'

Silence. I was already imagining her face when I saw her tonight. 'You know it's wrong to steal.'

'Yes.'

'So why do it?'

Silence. Maybe I could run away after school. 'Do you need money?'

'No.'

'Does your mother give you pocket money?' 'Yes.'

'You get pocket money each week?' 'Yes.'

'So why steal?'

Silence. Where could I run to? Where?

'Paul, is there anything that is upsetting you at home?' 'No, no.'

Silence. Maybe I could hide in the cloakroom. Wait there until everyone had gone. 'Paul,' Mr Snow said, 'if you don't say anything...'

His voice trailed off. I looked at my shoes and noticed the white scuff on the toes from playing football. I was getting quite good at the game now. And this one of cat and mouse too.

'So everything is fine at home? Yes?'

'Yes, Mr Snow.' Then silence. My head was bowed and my tongue silent.

'Okay, Paul, off you go.'

That night, it was nine minutes past eight o'clock when the meal finished and the sound of knives scraping against china plates stopped, and spoons finally settled into round bowls. Mrs K. took a napkin and wiped her small, bitter lips. Then she cleared her throat.

'Paul, clear the table. Bill, get the cane from the shed,' she said simply.

Bill's face assumed instant lines of disbelief. His head fell towards his left shoulder as if to say, 'No, not this. Don't make me do this.'

Mrs K. totally ignored his signals. 'Come on, Paul, take the dishes to the sink and please try not to smash any.'

I stood up and stacked the plates on each other and walked to the sink. Bill remained sitting, staring at his unconcerned wife. I returned to the table, stacked the dessert bowls and walked to the sink. Bill remained sitting and staring.

I returned again, stacked the remaining large dishes carefully into each other and walked to the sink. Bill stayed sitting.

When I started collecting the glasses Mrs K. said tightly, 'Bill, get me that cane now. Right now.'

I heard the sound of the chair screeching against the stone floor, the exaggerated sigh and the shaking of the head and then Bill was gone, out into the winter night.

'Paul,' Mrs K. said softly, 'get a cloth and wipe the table down.'

I walked to the sink and reluctantly walked back. Mrs K. sat still in her chair, her stern gaze upon me.

As I was finishing my cleaning, Bill came back in. He had in his hand a long, thin bamboo stick. I went to the sink and as I put the cloth down in the sink, I heard Mrs K. say, 'Paul, I want you in here right now.'

I walked back into the room.

'Take down your trousers,' she ordered. 'Right now.' Her voice was firm, irreproachable in its purpose.

'Now bend over that table.'

As I did so, again it struck me – that feeling that somehow this was right; that I had been chosen for this life, this moment.

'Bill,' Mrs K. said, nodding towards me. She wore a green jumper and a long tartan skirt. The stripes on it were brown and white. There was a huge pin on one side. I remember looking at it and wondering, 'Does that hold the skirt up?'

I received six lashes.

'If I ever catch you stealing from me again,' she snarled, 'you'll get double that amount. Now go.'

And that night in bed, my hands bandaged, a rubber sheet underneath me, I listened to the branch of the tree outside knock repeatedly on my window, as if the Devil himself wanted to come in. In that very moment I knew without doubt that the world had abandoned me. On that winter's night, I lost faith. I actually felt it vanish from inside of me. I was trapped, totally alone and I could not escape. I had no love, no belief and only fear inside me.

What I now realise is that this is how my real mother must have felt every night she went to bed.

And then Mrs K. was gone. Told me so herself. 'I'm leaving.' Six months in India. Working for *She* magazine as a journalist.

'You will miss me, won't you?' she commanded. I couldn't believe my luck. Six months, six whole months. A summer eternity. When I think of that time now the only image that my mind conjures up is that of diving into cool, cool water. The day my foster mother left me was the happiest day of my childhood. From dark came the light, from ugly came the beauty. I was free.

I played, I ran, I smiled. I lay on my back in the garden on sunny afternoons and gazed at the blue sky for hours, trying to read the shape of deep, puffy white clouds. I thought of God, I thought of Heaven and as I did there were no raised voices shouting at me, no raised hands to flinch from. I spent hours looking at trees, marvelling how they exploded out of the ground. They entranced me.

Better still, I came home from school and no one stood me in front of a mirror, like Mrs K. would, and said, 'Look at your dirty blazer, your dirty knees, you filthy boy.'

They said, 'Hello, Paul, home early. Go and wash yourself and then we'll have something to eat.'

I saw smiles on everyone around me. Even Bill cheered up. I kicked a ball around the garden, shouting to myself. 'Here comes George Best…past one…past two – goal!' No one told me to shut up and not be so stupid. They just hung clothes on the line and smiled indulgently at me. I devoured my books, safe in the knowledge that I could sink into them, fully submerge myself in their stories and not have to worry that any minute my cruel, twisted mother would demand I did some homework or raked the garden. I read Greek myths and saw Hercules clean the stables and kill Medusa. I imagined the Gods, powerful and potent, and wished they still lived so they could intervene, change my fortunes, forever. For finally I had a childhood.

I remember Mrs K.'s mother sat me on her knee in her car and let me move the wheel as we chugged along an empty Bagshot road. I was given money to buy sweets. I wasn't afraid to talk, wasn't afraid that I would be humiliated every time I opened my mouth. Mealtimes were busy with people talking. Afterwards, no one screamed at me to do my homework because I was a lazy, worthless so-and-so who needed all the education I could get – though 'God knows why anyone would want to take you on at their school.'

I ate ice cream; I kicked a football; I was a child. I was nine years old and a part of the world.

And then Mrs K. came home and she was not happy.

To accompany the series of articles that she gave to *She*, the magazine sent a photographer around to take a picture of the family. We posed in the dining room. The photographer said to Mrs K., 'Your son must have missed you very much.'

'Oh very much,' she replied, 'very much.'

There was a silence as I sat there blankly, both adults waiting for me to confirm her statement. After the photographer left, sent on his way by Mrs K.'s usual warm goodbyes to people heading out into the world, she turned to me and snarled, 'Get to your room now and think yourself lucky that I don't cane you.'

Somehow she had sensed the warmth that her absence had allowed to flourish within the house, she had sniffed out our happiness and we would now pay for our treachery – or rather, I would be forced to take the punishment. She began cooking hot curries, curries that scalded my mouth with every mouthful, curries so hot I would lunge for water to soothe my burning tongue.

'You're only allowed one glass of water,' she would then say. 'And you're not allowed to leave the table until every last scrap of food is off your plate.'

Most evenings after supper, I was left alone at the table with a half-empty plate and a dirty-coloured glass of water in which pieces of rice and beef floated like dead fish. A new regime had been instilled, harsher than ever before. I was to study every night and at weekends, although I would be allowed one TV show a week. I chose *Batman*. Pow! Wham! Zap! She laughed out loud at my choice. 'Typical of your low intelligence,' she sneered. I feared her even more now. No longer was I being treated as if Haileybury and Oxford were our shared ambitions.

She banned me from talking to anyone outside the house. Early one Sunday night, as I was kicking a ball around the garden and the light faded around me, a boy about my age and size came to the fence and said, 'Hello.'

He had just moved in next door and had a ball at his feet. He wanted to play. So did I. Mrs K. was cooking in the kitchen and often peered out to check on me. I couldn't take the risk. I ran past him and ignored him. When I passed him again, he said, 'Hello,' but in a slightly louder voice. Again, I ignored him. On the third time around, he half shouted at me. 'Hello.' I saw the puzzlement on his face. He thought I couldn't hear him.

I hissed at him, 'I can't talk, I'm not allowed.' And as I swept past him again, the bewildered look on that young boy's friendly face was forever burnt into my memory.

But the worst thing she did at this time, the absolutely worst thing, was when she sat me down and said, 'I am taking you out of school. I am going to teach you myself. Won't that be good?'

Here in my room, my lonely, lonely room with its ugly dark-brown chest of drawers and its small window which the tree knocks against, like some evil urgently signalling to come in, I walk with Hercules and sail the seven seas. I live inside the Trojan horse and I cut off the head of Medusa. I am Homer, the writer. Now I am Mark Twain, fishing down by the river with Huckleberry Finn. I am friends with the Fantastic Four and fly around the world with Thor. I am George Best. I score a thousand goals and I am in Sgt. Pepper's Lonely Hearts Club Band. I am Zeus and the world is mine. I am King

Agamemnon and I command a thousand troops. I am Stan
Lee and I draw all the Marvel comics.

Here in my room, my lonely, lonely room, I am everybody
except me because 'me' is no good. Me is stupid and silly and
worthless and gets the cane and gets screamed at. So here in
my room, my lonely, lonely room, I am everybody else until
the lock on the door clicks open and the real world walks
back into my life.

In my files it reports that I exasperate Mrs K. She says to
my social worker, 'You never know what is going on inside
his head.'

On my last day at The Manor school I stole a sixpence
from Mrs K.'s purse. On my last day at school there were no
lessons, just playing with my classmates in the playground
for the very last time but playing those games with tears
bubbling behind my eyes. Although I didn't know it at the
time, my removal from school was all Mr Frith's fault. I was
unaware that he had made moves to have me taken away from
Mrs K. I had no idea he was planning to adopt me. I had
no idea he wanted to rescue me because every day at school
he looked into me and sensed things were not quite right. I
didn't know that Mrs K. had then discovered his plans and
had immediately had me removed from his clutches as quickly
as possible. But I blessed his name the day I found out and
I bless it still for his efforts on my behalf. On my last day at
school, I shook hands with all my teachers. On my last day at
school I walked out of the gates smiling. Then, on the train
home, I went to the toilet, locked the door, pulled down the
lavatory seat and when I was sure that no one could hear me,
I sat down and spilled tears – all on my last day at school.

Now Mrs K. was my teacher, my life turned darker, more
dangerous. The day would start with a menial task – peeling
potatoes or vegetables, digging in the garden. I was allowed

a little play-time – which I spent, as ever, pretending to be George Best – and then it was back into the dining room with its stone floor to practise my handwriting, Mrs K.'s stern gaze hovering over me.

At one o'clock proper, the lessons began. Mrs K. would turn on the radio and sit with me at the table. A documentary, a different subject each day, would be broadcast and we would sit and listen to it in absolute silence. At its conclusion, she would turn off the radio and then say to me, 'Right, Paul, what did you learn?'

She would then test me on what had been said. My problem was that only five minutes into the lesson my mind would start wandering. I was worrying so much about remembering everything, I forgot it all. The programme would finish at one thirty and by one thirty-five I would be in absolute disgrace for not recalling a thing. 'Can't you remember anything that is said to you? Are you deaf as well as stupid?' I would sit there for this exasperated tirade of abuse and humiliation and pray that she wouldn't reach for the cane. A lot of the times my prayers were answered. A couple of times they weren't.

Mrs K. [reveals one report] described her own childhood as affectionless and loveless. She was a nuisance to her father as he was not fond of children. The mother tended to sympathise with the father rather than the daughter. The final rift with her mother occurred six years ago. It had its basis in a major row about Mrs K.'s upbringing of Elizabeth. Since then, Mrs K. and her mother have only seen each other about three times.

And then there were the moments – occasional, but I do recall them – when I would look up from my labours and see Mrs K., her face thin and pale, her expression shot through with some inner worry, some inner pain, sitting there with her long slim fingers clasped around a small china cup, wearing a

green woollen V-neck jumper and a tartan skirt, gazing out at
the garden, absolutely lost in her reverie. I never felt pity for
her, just puzzlement and a real hope that, in such a reflective
mood, her rage would be stilled.

One day, I went to confession.

'Forgive me, Father, for I have sinned.'

'How long is it since your last confession, my son?' 'A
week, Father.'

'And what sins do you have to tell me?'

The trouble was, I had none. I couldn't think of anything.
I had not stolen or sworn or hurt anyone. I had been a good
boy. Really and truthfully. So I sat there in the darkened box,
looking at the vague figure of a face expectantly waiting
behind the grille. I couldn't let him down so I made some
sins up.

'I stole sweets, Father. And I swore at my friend.' 'Is
that all?'

'Yes, Father.'

'Our Lord Jesus often spoke about the evil of stealing that
which belongs to another. To steal is a terrible thing. And so
is to use nasty words against others. You will say three Our
Fathers and two Hail Marys.'

'Yes, Father.' 'Now go in peace.'

I came out of the box and knelt on the hard wooden
pew. I began praying quickly and as I did I suddenly realised
something; by lying to Father Tucker in confession I had just
committed a huge sin.

Every day it was the same routine of trying so hard to get
my lessons right and always stumbling, always being shouted
at. Sometimes I was caned and screamed at for crying. On
other days I would be sent to my bedroom in disgrace only to
be called down a couple of hours later and served hot curry
for tea as Mrs K. sat with her husband and told him again

and again what an incompetent fool I was. As her teaching
failed to make me sparkle, the exasperation that Mrs K. felt
at my poor performances started to affect her. I was her
experiment and the results were not what she craved. The
path she wanted to push me down – Haileybury and Eton
and Oxford – was shrinking into the distance day by day. I
was too scared to learn and she was too angry to help me.
There was no way I would be accepted into this world. I
knew it and so did she. I was an experiment in failure. She
wrote another letter to Social Services. Within a month, her
wishes were granted. A young baby called Andrew arrived
at the house. He was dark-skinned, quiet. Two weeks later,
another child arrived. Caroline. She was light-skinned, lively.
The new recruits had arrived and I now knew my days were
numbered. And it scared me. For where would I go? I knew
the procedure, especially when I was told that I would now
be attending a very minor public school in Staines. So minor,
I forget its name.

In one of the final reports on a visit made by my social
worker, he states that Mrs K. is definitely 'having ambivalent
feelings' towards me. 'She sometimes thinks that perhaps he
ought to leave them now...' Mr K. is not so involved but the
social worker picks up on his ambivalence. He writes, 'I had
the impression that he would like to see Paul go although he
did not put this in so many words. I am not quite certain if
he is jealous of Paul and of Mrs K.'s involvement with him.'

I kissed a girl for the very first time during my brief stay at
my new school. She was blonde and her name was Maxine. I
came into class one day and the boy who sat next to me said,
'Maxine fancies you. She does. She told me.'

I looked over at her. To my surprised delight she was
smiling at me. The teacher had not yet arrived.

'Thanks,' I said to the boy.

I stood, walked over to Maxine, bent down, kissed her on the cheek and walked back to my desk. The teacher arrived just as I was sitting down.

'Sir,' said the boy sitting next to me, 'when you weren't here, Paul kissed Maxine Davis.'

'He did what?'

So now I started getting the cane at school as well as at home.

Unlike The Manor with its routine and rituals, my new school was overcrowded and run by an ageing man whose tenuous grip on reality created a freefall mood that infected everyone in the building. His wayward approach had its disadvantages. You were caned for the most minor of offences. At other times, though, it was great, especially when he cancelled lessons in the afternoon for no reason whatsoever and insisted we play football instead. His decisions to do so coincided with Mrs K.'s adoption of a more relaxed approach as her attentions now turned to the new arrivals, Andrew and Caroline. On occasions she would even shock me by asking how my day had been.

'My teacher says I should do well in my exams,' I would lie to her, 'and my pals call me George Best.' (They didn't, but I thought it might sound good.)

'Oh,' she would reply. 'That's nice.' I might as well have said it in Italian for all she understood. I was now the Forgotten Boy. It was not that she had fully tempered her behaviour since Andrew and Caroline's arrival; there were still outbursts of anger, frightening in their intensity – only there seemed to be less of them. I looked at Andrew and Caroline at the dinner table and resented their innocence.

For my part, I was still heavily stealing, but not from home. Instead, I was robbing shops of everything I could get my hands on. On one occasion, I walked into a sweet shop near where we lived, picked up a whole box of Batman cards in front of everyone in the shop and then walked outside. The owner, a middle-aged man, followed me out with a bemused look.

'What are you doing?' he asked gently. He wasn't angry or raging. He was just curious that this little boy thought he could get away with something so brazen. Through the window I could see a couple of mothers staring at me. I stood there silently, holding the box filled with the sweet packets. I had no idea what to say because I had no idea what I was doing.

'Give them back to me,' he said softly. I handed them over and a little smile crossed his lips. I turned away and walked to the train station to go to school. That night, Mrs K. was waiting for me. I had just got changed from my school clothes when I heard her voice summoning me to the kitchen. She sat at the light-brown wooden table and as soon as I walked in and felt the room's temperature I knew my crime had been reported. Probably one of the two women in the shop. I'd vaguely recognised one of them.

'You've just got changed,' she said, a bright tone in her voice to begin with.

'Yes.'

'Now take off your clothes.' 'Sorry?'

'I said, take off your clothes.'

To the right of her, leaning against the windowsill, was the bamboo cane. I took off my T-shirt.

'Put it there,' she said, gesturing to the table.

I leant over and placed it on the wooden surface.

'That's right. Now your trousers.'

Through the dining-room window I could see the boy next door. He was kicking a ball around the garden. Then I saw another boy come into view and they began kicking the ball to each other. I prayed that they wouldn't glance over and see me standing in just my socks and underpants.

'Now the rest of your clothes.'

I pulled down my pants and stepped out of them. I lifted one leg up, pulled off a sock, then the other. 'Now come to the table,' Mrs K. said, standing up, 'and bend over. I am going to teach you never to steal again.' There is a moment that everyone who has been caned knows all too well. It is that agonising period of time between bending down and receiving the first blow on your cheeks, a moment when you are caught in a state of absolute dread of the pain you know will soon be yours.

It was in that moment, as I lay with my face to one side on the table, that I thought to myself, I am a better footballer than both those boys playing outside. I bet you I am. I bet you.

One of our teachers announced that after school on Friday there would be a trip to the swimming pool. All of my class seemed to be going. I went home and asked Mrs K., 'Can I go swimming after school?'

She said, 'No, I want you home by five. Now go to the study and do your homework.'

I went to the study and put out my books in front of me. Latin. I had Latin homework. For an hour I sat and stared at my books. Why couldn't I go swimming? Everyone else was going. Why not me? It wasn't much to ask for. It was with the school. That was all. Swimming, we were going swimming. I picked up a book and started to read it but the words made no sense and the question wouldn't stop bouncing around my head. My whole life was Latin.

The next day I secretly placed my swimming trunks and a towel in my satchel. At school I sat daydreaming through morning lessons. I played football that afternoon, and then joined my class and we all went to the swimming pool with our teacher. Like all little boys and girls do. I came home an hour later than normal. I walked into the kitchen through the back door. Mrs K. stood by the oven. She was busy stuffing mincemeat into a large marrow. She stopped, looked at me and said, 'Open your satchel.'

I did so. Inside were my sodden towel and trunks. I didn't care. On the way home I had already imagined the impending caning. At the very least there would be a beating, a smack around the head, a torrent of abuse to deal with.

Instead, I got nothing. Nothing at all. She just looked at me and said with a tone of ice, forged in utter resignation, 'I have tried my best. We all have.' Then she carried on preparing the evening meal.

I didn't know it but at that moment, as I stood in the kitchen alone with my wet hair and sodden brown satchel, the six-year experiment to turn me into that which I was not, and never ever could be, had finally ended. I had two days left with Mrs K. and then I would never see her again. Except in my nightmares or when I was alone and busy hurting myself.

* * *

Many years ago, a young girl was sitting in her classroom when a message arrived. The headmistress wanted to see her. Urgently. The girl, a loner by nature, not popular but intelligent, rose from her studies and went to the dusty office where her Head sat waiting.

'I have terrible news for you,' the Head said gravely. 'Your step-brother has been killed in an air crash.' At which point the young girl started howling hysterically. It was a wailing sound of pain but as it gathered pace, strangely it became laughter but laughter that was cruel and exultant. The Head said it was the shock. But it wasn't. For what the Head didn't know was that the girl was filled with jealousy for the brother she had inherited from her father's first marriage. She obsessed over him. He got all the attention, he got all the love. He was brilliant. He had been to Haileybury. He had received first-class honours at Oxford. He had joined the RAF and earned himself the DFC and the bar. The girl was given none of these chances. She was neglected, left alone, abandoned because of this brilliant young man and his flying machine. And now he was gone, gone forever. Oh happy day. Oh happy, glorious day.

When the girl left school, she went into journalism and later publishing. She married a weak man named Bill and she prospered. But her stepbrother haunted her all the time, haunted her and taunted her from beyond the grave. ('I was the one they loved. You weren't.') And so she decided to take a child and remake him in his image. The child, carefully selected, would follow his path: Haileybury and Oxford and then into the RAF. Of this, the girl was absolutely determined. Nothing would stand in her way.

Later on, some would say that this girl loved her brother so much that it was this that spurred her on into trying to recreate him. But it wasn't love that drove her, it was revenge. This girl, this skinny girl with the pale ring and the thin face, wanted revenge for the isolation she had suffered. She needed to avenge the lack of love and warmth from her father.

And so when she laid that child naked over a table to beat him with a stick or when she swooped down to scream at him and make him so nervous that he had to retreat inside himself or when she tied his hands at night and locked him in his room and scared him to his very soul, she was not seeing or hearing that child. She only saw her brother, her hated brother's face, the face she could not erase from her mind.

It was my terrible luck to be that child. It was scandalous that those who should have known better did not see through the veneer of respectability that this girl fooled most of them with. 'Gracious living': to live in fear every day of my childhood, to have my very soul attacked by this deranged woman and to live with the consequences to this day; gracious living, I spit on you.

But not any longer. The experiment was over and so was my time with Mrs K. As I lay in my locked bedroom that night in darkness and pain, a phone call was being made. I was no longer wanted in the house. I was no longer of use to Mrs K.

I was officially about to become an orphan.

Five

In Purgatory

May 1968

On a cool Sunday evening in the early summer of 1968, a small Austin car slowly crunched its way up our drive and came to a halt. The doorbell was rung. I was sitting in the kitchen, alone. I heard my name called. I stood up and, with unease as my only companion, slowly walked into the hallway. Mrs K. stood facing the open door. Her right arm was extended outwards and her long fingers were pressed hard against the door's top, thus forming a bridge. Behind her, a young couple were loitering in the driveway. I could see a suitcase, brown and small, in the man's large hands. The people she had always threatened to call when I was bad had finally, finally arrived. Mrs K. was avoiding all eye contact. It was the first time I had ever seen her so unsure.

'Off you go,' she said lightly, her eyes motioning to the outside. The couple turned and I walked under Mrs K.'s arm and into the fading sunlight. I settled in the back seat of the car and as it reversed down the drive I saw the door of the house slowly shut. The car turned into College Lane. I resisted the temptation. I didn't look back at the house that had served as a terrible kind of home to me for so many years. Instead, I now realised that I had no idea where I was going or what was happening. I was sat in silence, with two strangers. In a moving car.

'Okay,' the young man said brightly, looking at me in his mirror as the car gathered pace. I said nothing, just moved my shoulders, stared at the colours flashing by my window. 'I suppose you're wondering where you're going,' the woman said, turning towards me. Their breezy voices annoyed me. I kept my gaze upon the passing scenery. I didn't bother replying. I was beyond caring. I was out of the terror but into the unknown.

An hour later the car pulled up at a large house named Woodrough, in Bramley, near Guildford. It was besieged by greenery on all sides. I didn't know – but would soon find out – that this large building was a halfway house, a place where the county council put children whilst they figured out what to do with them. On the doorstep, I saw a portly man with curly hair and glasses looking curiously at us. I got out of the car and walked, behind the couple, towards him. I heard the man say, 'This is Paul,' and then he moved aside to let me through. I walked forward and stopped.

The portly man looked down at me, nodded and removed the pipe from his mouth. 'Come in,' he gently said. And with those words I was delivered unto care. The couple handed him the suitcase. Then they slowly walked back to the car. I hadn't said a word to them.

'My name is John Brown,' the man with the pipe said, standing back to allow me to walk into a small hallway with a staircase to the right and a sitting room to the left. 'I'm in charge here. Are you hungry? Would you like something to eat?'

I shook my head. Everything felt unreal. There was nothing tangible to grip onto. Food was unnecessary in such a state.

'Well, let's get you washed and then I'll show you to your bed.'

He walked up the stairs and led me into a long bathroom where five slightly off-white sinks were fixed to a wall. He handed me a towel, reached over and turned on the taps. I stripped down to my underwear with no shame whatsoever. As I washed, he began the questions. What had happened? Why was I here? Had I done something bad? Why had my parents let me go? As he spoke, I realised that he was as surprised as I was to be in this situation. The questions continued. But as they fell around my head in vain, the strangest thing suddenly occurred. From out of nowhere, I felt the whole of my body freeze, but not on the outside – on the inside. This strange sensation started at my stomach and it rushed to my head. It was unlike anything I had ever experienced, like being injected with an anaesthetic which numbs and kills every emotion. A deep layer of ice, vast and strong, had been created inside me; that's the nearest I can get to describing the feeling. It would take years for me to start breaking it down. I stared at the water dropping into the sink. I felt the rush of ice inside of me settle. I now looked up at John, standing there, looking at me with concerned kindness and I coldly replied, 'I don't know, you'll have to ask my foster mother.' And that's what I kept repeating to his every question, 'I don't know. You'll have to ask her.'

It was the first time in my life that I had stood up to an adult stranger, the first time I had not acquiesced to an elder's wants. It's why I remember it so well.

I was led to a bedroom where three other boys lay sleeping. I got into bed. As I did the idea that I was on the verge of becoming another person altogether ran into my mind and shone briefly. Then the darkness came, and with it a new world, a new understanding.

The next day a strange woman woke me. She said, 'Come on, time to get up. Get dressed and washed and then come down to breakfast.' She was tall, thin and wore glasses. Her hair was unruly, curly grey. She was John's wife, Molly, and she looked like how I imagined other people's aunts to look. John and Molly ran the Home together with other staff to assist them with the running of the house. I slowly dressed, cleaned my teeth in the bathroom and went down the stairs where the noise of children eating and talking guided me towards a small dining room. I walked in and faced three tables, with adults and children of all ages at each one. On the far right-hand side of the room there was a window that looked out onto a spacious garden.

'Paul, sit here.' It was John, motioning me towards his table. I sat next to him and as I positioned myself on the chair I keenly felt everyone's eyes upon me.

'Did you sleep all right?' he enquired. I nodded.

'Have some cereal, some toast.'

I ate four slices, thick with marmalade. I would never have dared to ask for so much at Mrs K.'s, let alone eat it.

When I finished the toast, I sat with my head bowed, wondering what to do next.

'I'd like you to come with me,' John said quietly and he stood up. All the boys and girls, from the young to the teenaged, watched again as I followed him out across the hallway and into the sitting room.

He motioned towards a chair and I sat down. John sat on the edge of his seat.

'You may be wondering what's…eh…happening,' he began slowly. He vaguely gestured around the room with his pipe. 'This house is called Woodrough. You have been placed in care. As is the case with all the children here, you'll stay here until it's decided where you will live on a more permanent basis.'

He paused. 'Do you know what it means to be in care?' 'Yes,' I quickly lied.

He didn't reply immediately, just looked at me and puffed thoughtfully on his pipe.

'In a week or two, the school we have which is at the bottom of the drive will open and you'll go there every day. In the meantime, why don't you go out into the garden and play with the other children.'

I stood and as I left the room he said, 'Don't worry, you'll be looked after here.'

I sat in a tree. For a week I sat in a tree. While the other children noisily played beneath, I sat eight feet in the air and stared directly into the dark dining room opposite me. I spent hours doing this. Every morning, the same routine: rise, wash, dress, breakfast and then go out to climb the garden's only tree and sit on a branch, mournful, sad, disconnected to all around me. A black cloud had settled in my head and I had no way of losing it. I felt nowhere. I didn't speak to the kids around me and they in turn ignored me. I only spoke to John or Molly if I was spoken to, otherwise I was silent.

Occasionally, as I sat upon my branch, John Brown would appear at the dining-room window, pipe in hand and look right at me. I would simply stare back. Then he would move away. It killed me that he never came out and asked what the matter was. I took him to be kind, understanding. So why wasn't he asking me what the problem was? Why didn't he come to me? Why didn't John Brown take away my sadness? Everything was so unfair.

And then the Painterman arrived.

I can't remember his proper name now but he came dressed in white overalls that befitted his title. He had a rough energy, a brusque style, and I thought he was wonderful. He spoke of wondrous, glamorous things. He gave the impression to me that nothing in life was a problem. Everything was achievable. After Mrs K.'s strict regime, his attitude absolutely fascinated me. When I was with him I forgot the oppressive cloud in my head. He said girls were easy to kiss – he'd kissed a million. He said becoming a footballer was easy. I told him that the kids at my last school called me George Best.

'What's your real name?' he asked. 'It's important, this.'

I told him, Paul, although, I added, I wasn't sure now.

'Why?' he asked, applying his brush to the wall with a vigour I can still see. In the corner stood his paint-splattered black radio playing the number-one record of the day, Louis Armstrong's 'What a Wonderful World.'

Because, I explained, I didn't live with my foster mother any more and she had given me the name.

'But your real mother must have called you something.'

Of course, my mother had called me Paolo, Paolo Hewitt. I had forgotten all about it. Years ago, I had actually mislaid my own name, buried it in the darkness of my mind. Now I could retrieve it, now it could be used. It was good to know this, to assume a new identity, to start life again as someone else. Paolo Hewitt, that's who I now was.

'Paolo Hewitt,' I said with a kind of wonderment.

The Painterman stopped work, put down his brush and turned his sharp blue eyes upon me. 'Let's see then,' and he reached into his overalls and pulled out a worn-down pencil and a grubby pad that had figures and symbols scrawled on its first page. As he wrote, he said out aloud, 'Poor Low Hewitt.' Then he turned the paper and showed me what he had written. It was my name, spelt Paulo Hewitt.

'If you're going to be a famous footballer,' he announced, 'the name is important. Really important. A good name and you're on your way and Poor Low Hewitt [he nodded his head encouragingly here] – not a bad name.'

And this is how I was given a new name at ten years of age. It's also how I misspelled the damn thing for the next twelve years of my life.

The Painterman, he spoke again of women. 'That Sandra, you should go for her,' he said encouragingly. Sandra was about thirteen with shortish hair and a foggy look that she wore upon her face most days, as if she was just passing through life and onto a far more important destination. I had been gripped by that look since the day I saw her. The Painterman's word was now my law. He was right, I should go for her.

I began looking over at her during mealtimes. When she went into the playroom to play table tennis, I followed, sat in a corner, pretending to read a book. All the time I studied her. I wanted her kiss. I told the Painterman I didn't know what to say to her and he replied, 'Don't worry, your chance will come.' And, as ever, the Painterman was right.

School had opened now and I couldn't take it seriously. 'School' was a small hut built in a clearing by the right-hand side of the drive's entrance. It had some desks and chairs but no blackboard. It had been built because the headmaster at the local school had announced he wouldn't take orphans. Simple as that. Perhaps he thought we were diseased. The council had to provide for us and so a middle-aged woman, who was probably as gripped as we were by its utter pointlessness, would open up at nine o'clock and make us read and write. I did little of either, just stared at the back of Sandra's head, the light-brown hair that lay thick upon her shoulders.

One night in the bedroom, Billy, the eldest of the boys, announced that in the afternoon, he and Sandra had gone behind a hedge near the school and she had shown him her knickers. 'Pink, they were,' he said with a flourish. Instantly, raging jealousy reared up and pierced my heart. I turned over onto one side. I didn't want Billy to see the heat of my wound. I didn't ever want to talk to him.

Two days later, during a lunchtime break, Sandra called me over. She was sitting on a small wall in the driveway. It was a sunny day and, behind her, shafts of sunlight cut through the trees. She looked utterly amazing. In her hand she held a copy of *She* magazine. 'I've got something to show you,' she cooed. 'Look.' Sandra turned the magazine towards me and there was the picture the photographer had taken of Mrs K. and her 'family.' I stared at the photograph, examined myself standing glumly next to Mrs K.'s false smile and bitterly recalled the extreme unhappiness of it all.

'It's you. You're in a magazine.'

Of course, Sandra had no idea of the picture's true meaning. To her it was exciting. In those days if you had your picture published in a magazine it really was a big deal. It wasn't to me. Nothing was a big deal to me. Still, her excitement encouraged me. I now saw my chance. I stood above her. She was wearing a skirt that stopped just short of her knees. What would it take for her just to pull it up? She had already performed this act for Billy, maybe even more times for others I didn't know about.

'Show us your knickers.'

'No,' she replied, as if I had said something really stupid, not even worth her consideration.

'Please. Just once.'

'No,' she said, brightly. 'Look – your picture in a magazine.' I ignored her.

'Show us your knickers, please.'

Surely, it wasn't a lot to ask for? I didn't want to touch or kiss, just look. 'Go on. Just pull your skirt up.' That's all I wanted.

'No,' she angrily replied. Then she stood up and handed me the magazine. 'I don't do that for anyone.'

'But you showed Billy,' I shouted after her. I took the magazine and dropped it on the ground. I walked away. I never mentioned Sandra again to the Painterman and when he brought up the subject I just told him that she was ugly. So bloody ugly.

One Sunday I walked to church. I was still a daydream believer. I was sitting in the pews when Father Tucker walked in to commence mass. I couldn't believe it. It was like seeing a ghost. My old priest, there in front of me. I stared at him for the whole hour wondering if he had seen me. Salvation, I sensed, was near. After mass, I waited for him outside the church. Priests traditionally appear at the door after mass, wishing their congregation well as they depart to further sin. When he came out onto the church steps, he spotted me straight away.

'Paul,' he said pleasantly.

I couldn't help it. One look at his jowly, kindly face was enough. I felt hot tears literally explode out of me. I ran into his arms and buried my crying face into his cassock. I heard him say, 'Oh now, oh now – no need to cry, surely,' and I felt the warm circle of his hand pat my head. At that precise moment, I wanted to tell him all. I wanted him to see the big hurt inside of me and take it away forever. I wanted the misery lifted from my soul. I wanted the cloud in my head to go away. I wanted him to take me away and put me in his safe, warm world where I could hide from everything. That's what I wanted more than anything else.

Father Tucker kept patting me on the head as I sobbed into his cassock. 'There, there. Come on, come with me.'

Then he led me into the church and into the vestry. I stood in front of him as he slipped off his cassock and put on his dark jacket. 'I'm glad the tears have stopped,' he said. 'Do you live near here now?'

I nodded. 'A home called Woodrough.'

He nodded as if he was already aware of this fact. 'And your mother?'

I shrugged my shoulders.

'I see,' he said, 'I see.' He had lost none of his ability to comfort with gentleness. He put his arm over my shoulder and led me towards his car. We got in and we drove off. Now that my rush of tears had finished I found that I was struggling to express myself. It wasn't just Woodrough and where I lived that pained me. It was the years and years of hurt I wanted to tell him about. But where to start? Where to start? I felt helplessness grip the inside of my throat. I didn't have the words to use or the heart to tell him. But that was okay. Soon, we would be at Father Tucker's house and he would give me sandwiches and I would eat them and then we would sit in his garden and the sun would shine and the sky would be blue and I would drink lemonade and he would save me.

Father Tucker steered his car around a corner and with a jolt I realised that he was now taking a right and starting the slow drive up towards Woodrough. I couldn't believe it. I thought we were going back to his house where I would be saved. By Father Tucker. But we weren't and, of course, I was too meek to protest. Father Tucker brought the car to a halt. 'Go in, Paul,' he said, 'and I'll see you next Sunday.' And with those words I was delivered again into care.

I went back to mass every Sunday after that. But Father Tucker never again took mass in that church. And I never saw him again.

At Woodrough, there were three meals a day to attend: breakfast, lunch and tea. The day's first meal began at eight. Lunch was at one o'clock and tea at five. One day, at half past twelve, John Brown unexpectedly called me in from the garden. I was kicking a ball around on my own pretending to be George Best. I was also secretly hoping that one of the kids would ask me for a game.

'Paulo,' he shouted, 'I need you.'

I kicked the ball into a hedge and walked over to him. He ushered me into the sitting room. We weren't usually allowed into the house until lunch was called.

'The cricket has started,' he explained simply. Then he settled down to watch the television with his pipe. I sat next to him and together we watched the game for half an hour. He called no one else in, just me. He didn't explain himself and all he spoke of as we sat there was cricket. He told me who was playing, what players to take note of, how the game was played, how a Test series (which was what we were watching) worked. I found myself interested. The next day he again called me in; then the next day, until it was routine. I loved it. Just me and him and a cricket match. One day when we were watching my favourite batsman, Ken Barrington, play the West Indies, John said, still staring at the TV, 'I've got a treat for you. Someone special is coming to see you tomorrow.'

'Who's that?' I asked, concentrating on the game. 'Your mother,' he replied. 'Your real mother.'

The day I first met my mother, at ten years of age, was a strange day, a day of wondering and of curiosity, a day filled with possibility. Since the arranging of her visit, I had naturally assumed that John and Molly Brown would be present throughout my mother's stay, that they would guide me through this momentous occasion. I was also feeling very confused. What does one feel for a mother one has never

met? What? How was I supposed to act? Should I run crying
into her arms? Should I shake her hand? What should I call
her? Mother? I presumed I should feel something. This was
my mother, the most important person in my life, I had been
told. I searched inside myself for a reaction, but time and time
again nothing came to help me. Every time I considered the
meeting my mind went blank. Finally, I had to conclude that
my mother was not the most important person in my life.
She was an absolute stranger, a distant figure on a very large
horizon. I just prayed she would not see that it was so. To
add to the confusion, at the appointed hour a couple I had
never met before arrived at the house with a child in tow, a
small boy, fair-haired, and about my age. He was James, their
son. John Brown introduced me to them and then, to my
surprise, he said, 'They'll be looking after you now' and he
left the room. The man said they had organised a special trip
for a special day. They would be accompanying me with my
mother, not John or Molly.

Fifteen minutes later as we sat quietly in the sitting room
there was a distant noise, a gathering of voices and then in she
walked. My mother. 'Hello, Paul,' she cried, 'hello,' and she
came straight over and kissed me on the cheek. 'Hello, Paul,
hello,' she repeated loudly.

It was a high-pitched voice and jolly. She stood in front of
me clutching a handbag and she smiled down at me. Her face
had make-up on. She wore a dark-blue cardigan, a grey dress,
blue shoes. Her hair was grey and her eyes were small and
black. Her face was wrinkled from age but also from worry.

I said 'hello' back and, satisfied, she now reached inside
her bag and pulled out some sweets.

'For you, Paul, for you.'

I said thank you and she smiled back at me and then
looked for somewhere to sit. The woman who was now

looking after me stood and guided my mother to a seat where
she rested herself and then she looked back at me.

'Hello,' she said once more. 'Hello, Paul.'

My foster mother called me Paul. My own mother could
not know how much I hated that name.

They took us on this summer's day to a nearby lake. The
couple pulled out sandwiches and plates and cups and flasks.
I sat and ate with their son James and did so in silence. My
mother sat to the left of the couple. Every now and again
the woman would lean over and say, 'Everything okay, Mrs
Hewitt?', and she would smile and say, 'Yes, lovely,' and then
occasionally look over at me and say, 'Hello, Paul, hello.'
Then she would return to her daydreaming. I don't think the
drugs had got to her by then or she wouldn't have lasted the
afternoon. Years later she would arrive at my sister's house,
stay an hour and then say, 'I'd like to go home now,' and
firmly nod her head and say, 'Yes, we go now.' But on this
day of the mother-and-child reunion she sat dreamily lost
in herself, although she was always careful to pay attention
when needed.

'Hello, Paul, hello.'

And she made sure that no one, but no one, could tell
what thoughts were crowding her mind as she spent three
hours in the company of the son she lost ten years ago and for
whom she now had nothing but the briefest words.

In my files dated from this period, my social worker asks
John and Molly about my mother's visit. They tell him it went
fine but that I was more thrilled by my recent birthday present
from them – a football. They also held a party for me. I told
them that this was the first birthday party I had ever been
given. They did not believe me.

A week later, I started smoking.

It was Billy's fault, really. Billy was my new friend now that the Painterman had also deserted me, his painted walls and the memory of his advice the only real evidence I now had of his existence at Woodrough. Billy shared the same room as me and one day, after school, as we walked up the drive, he grabbed me and said, 'This way.' I followed him up the bank and into the woods. We found a clearing and he pulled out an open packet of Number Ten cigarettes. The box was red and white and dirty.

'Found them on the road outside,' he lied. He handed me a cigarette and rummaged for some matches.

'I've never smoked before,' I told him. I knew John would be annoyed if I did. But John wasn't there so I didn't care.

'Nothing to it,' Billy said. He put the fag in his mouth and expertly lit it. Then he struck another match and held it towards me. It took five matches to light my fag. When I finally pulled away, puffing, he cried, 'Take the smoke down, don't blow it out.' I managed three puffs in this manner and then the world went dizzy for a minute. When I recovered, Billy was smiling and I sensed a good familiarity between us. I saw my chance. I had to ask him. I'd been dying to for weeks.

'Billy,' I said, 'did Sandra really show you her knickers?'

He grinned. 'Yeah, she did,' he replied. He took another puff, inhaled deeply. 'You should have seen them. White, they were!' he said, still grinning.

I had settled. I liked Woodrough. I really liked John Brown. His gentleness and kindness reminded me of Father Tucker. I felt safe around him. I was drawn to his serene air, his utter contentment with life. I would watch cricket with him and then after lunch, under his gentle urging, I'd get the other kids to play. The game would fall apart after a few minutes because of thorough disinterest from the younger ones who had to field. Billy and I would then get a ball and play my favourite game: re-enacting famous goals. Usually by George Best.

Billy was wise. 'You weren't called George Best at school,' he sneered once.

'Yes, I was, that was my name.' 'No, it wasn't.'

At tea I would make a point of telling John Brown once more the story behind my glorious nickname. He would say, 'Well, I'm sure you deserved it,' and I would smile smugly at Billy who sat at another table taking no notice of me.

It didn't matter. For once, I was happy. This was how life was meant to be, I had come to realise. No violence, no tension, no anger. Just playing football and eating sandwiches and feeling the sun and making friends and enjoying the world. But it was a happiness tempered by one dark fact: the knowledge that at some point – as it had been explained a few times now – Woodrough would have to let me go. It was a temporary home. Nothing more. But this I refused to believe. I figured there was no way that John or Molly would let me leave. They were the parents I wanted so why couldn't I have them? I would be so happy to stay here. They could make an exception for me. 'I'm special. Remember?' There, the problem was solved.

But they did, they let me go. Because they had to.

In my files, the following is said of me at this time: 'undemonstrative, cold and deep, talkative and moody, lazy, slipshod, unreliable, a fluent liar, does not trust adults, is over-anxious to be in the gang and is easily led.' It also says I 'like mass because of its rather flamboyant nature' and that 'the Browns think I have made good progress since being at Woodrough.' Oh and apparently I am now able to take a joke against myself.

Again, a car came to take me away. I stood in the empty hallway, tears burning my throat. John and Molly walked in.

John ruffled my hair, 'Don't forget the cricket, eh?' and at that the tears splashed onto my face. I was taken outside and Molly lent down and gave me a little hug whilst John stood behind her, puffing on his pipe. They told me everything would be all right. Everybody did that.

I got into the car, bound again for another unknown destination. I felt helpless – because John Brown had been right. I had been looked after at Woodrough. I had been shown kindness and care. The Browns had started to wipe away the hurt. Now all of that was gone and, worse, I couldn't understand why. Surely, if I was happy...

The driver of my car leant over me and opened the dashboard. He pulled out a pack of Weights non-tipped cigarettes and lit one. He had a large stomach, a grey-tinged goatee beard and full, red cheeks. 'I hope I never catch you smoking one of these,' he said with a laugh that sounded vaguely threatening. I had just met Barry Isleworth, the man in charge of my new home.

Six

The Looked After Kids

September 1968

My new home (I was starting to lose count now) was painted white and was situated at the top of a small hill. It was possible to imagine both good and evil flourishing within its many rooms and it took me weeks to fully absorb myself into it, to feel safe within this new environment most of the time. I longed for Woodrough.

Outside, land surrounded the house on all sides and ran down to the roads. From this space, two gardens had been fashioned. There was the large garden where we mainly hung out – you reached it when you went through the front door, walked across the drive and onto some steps which led down onto the lawn, and to the left of the house there was another much smaller garden. Beyond it, land that had been placed out of bounds to us sloped down to the main road. In fact, most of this land had been put out of bounds because the bushes and trees made it impossible for staff to keep an eye on us. Living in such expansive surroundings was slightly unsettling. The grounds and the house itself were for rich people, people who ran large businesses, spoke in the Lords, read *The Times* and played golf on Saturdays. Yet it was inhabited by children stripped of many, many things; kids who were poor of soul, looked after by people who were underpaid.

'Bloody shit, bloody toss. Bloody, shit, prick, bloody, bloody.'

Me, on the phone to Mrs K., taking my revenge. Listening to this abuse, standing next to me and laughing his head off is Big Tommy. Big Tommy is the leader of the gang in the Home. There are five of us. Big Tommy is sixteen. Terry comes next, he's the fat one. Then there's Graham, the good dresser. He always wears black leather gloves even in summer, Big Tommy tells me. Then there's me, the youngest, and above all there is my new best mate, Jimmy B., who is slightly older than me.

I had been at the Home for three weeks and I was shedding another skin, looking to become a different person. Change was a must, a necessity to survive the whirlwind change that was my life now. I smoked, I swore and I was a thief again. I felt wilder. I was no longer 'Paul.' Paul was dead. Dead and buried. Instead, I was in a gang and in that gang I felt my future lay. Why? Because the guys in it made me feel good. When Jimmy B. smiled at me, it felt good. When Graham said to me, 'You're all right, you,' it felt good. When Big Tommy said to me, 'Why don't you ring up someone you hate and swear at them? What they going to do about it?' it felt absolutely right. It made me feel good to say all the swear words that I knew – 'Bloody, shit, bloody prick, bloody' – to a startled Mrs K. at the other end of the line. Fucking good.

'Paul, put the phone down.' 'Bloody, shit.'

'Paul, put the phone down now.' 'Bloody prick.'

The line went dead. I called her back. She left the phone ringing. 'Forget her,' Big Tommy said and moved away.

I walked proudly beside him. Normally, the gang walked according to its hierarchy which meant that the youngest members of it, Jimmy B. and I, brought up the rear. Not tonight. Big Tommy and I walked back to the utterly tedious and boring barn dance that we had been taken to (this was the staff's idea of what we would enjoy) together and I felt proud.

Big Tommy had muscles, curly hair, was tall and imposing. He frightened just about everyone. Even Barry, the man in charge, was careful around Big Tommy. One prod too far and he would wrap you up for good. That's why I proudly walked beside him. No one could touch me now. Not even Mrs K.

The next morning, after breakfast, Barry called me into the sitting room. Straight away, he asked me, 'Like making phone calls, do you?'

I blushed and quickly looked away. Barry's voice lifted itself in anger. 'Do you?' he half shouted. 'You like to make phone calls using disgusting language, do you?' He walked towards me and then leant down and placed his bearded face inches away from mine. It was a favoured trick of his. Lean down and shout into the kid's face. That puts the fear up them. He was right. I flinched fearfully. 'Did you call your mother last night? Did you?'

I could see the grey hairs in his dark goatee beard jutting out towards me, accusingly. I could feel his breath shave my face.

I had no choice. 'Yes,' I replied meekly, my head turned away from him, 'but she's not my mother.'

Barry ignored my semantics. It wouldn't be the last time he'd do that either. 'Think it's funny to use swear words?

Like swear words, do you? Think they make you tough or something? And where did you get those swear words from? Eh? You never knew any when you got here. So who taught you? Tommy? Graham? Terry? Jimmy? Eh? Your little gang.' That, I wouldn't answer. You never split on another. Golden rule of survival. Barry now stood up and looked down at me. His tone slightly softened. I was scared but I somehow knew he wouldn't hit me. His overwrought manner had convinced me of that.

'You do not make phone calls without my permission and you do not phone Mrs K. ever again. Okay?'

I nodded.

He stood looking at me and said, 'Go.' I walked out of the room and when I looked back he was sitting in a chair, smoking a cigarette and staring into nothing. Meanwhile, I went looking for my gang.

I had joined the gang the first week I was at the Home. I had arrived on a Saturday afternoon, distraught and hurt at having to leave Woodrough. I soon found out that the best places to go were the boiler room or the smallish area made up of bamboo sticks that lay at the back of the main garden. This area was a world within a world. This is where you smoked and took girls and hid from the Home and your life there.

Over the fence was the real world of student protests and the Rolling Stones urinating in petrol stations and Joe Cocker screaming 'With A Little Help From My Friends' and long hair outraging people and *2001: A Space Odyssey* and Vietnam and Chairman Mao. Out there the talk was about the future; an imagined world where people took little pills for their meals (after those mealtimes with the K.s I loved that idea) and wore white tunic suits and looked at each other as they spoke on the phone. But in the Home, we lived in a separate universe, hidden away, creating our own little worlds in the bamboo forest to protect us.

Branching off from the main drive, just before the house came into view, was another drive but on the left-hand side. This led you to the back of the house and an area known as the courtyard. It was where the washing was hung. Fixed to the wall on the side of the house was a pair of steps that led you down into a dark boiler room. This was where I and a thousand other kids smoked a million cigarettes. Inside the actual house there were three floors, seven bedrooms for staff and children, two sitting rooms, a dining room, a playroom, a cloakroom and a kitchen, where a cook, Mrs Willoughby, prepared her hot meals.

The boiler room was warm and after the bollocking I had just received from Barry, it was the place where I was now headed. I walked into the cold cloakroom where we hung our coats and placed our 'good' shoes (donated by persons unknown and worn to church, school and boring barn dances) in named wooden lockers. I opened the cloakroom door and walked out into the courtyard. I walked over and stood at the top of the steps that led down to the boiler room and I looked down. I could see a lit cigarette end being fired in the gloom. Good.

'Who is it?' I asked quietly.

Jimmy B.'s face appeared out of the gloom and motioned me down. I carefully went down the stairs. Every week, all the children, apart from the very young, were given duties, and maintenance of the boiler was one of them. It meant stoking up the fire last thing at night. It meant standing outside in the freezing cold shovelling coal into a strategically placed manhole. It meant it was a great place to have a cigarette and hide the fact because if any member of the staff smelled smoke on your breath, you simply replied, 'It must be from the boiler. That's my duty this week.'

Jimmy handed me his cigarette. He smoked like an old man. Hand cupped over it, drawing on it heavily. I took a puff. 'Fucking bastard,' I said.

'Barry?' 'Bloody prick.' 'Wanker.'

'I'm going to phone Mrs K. again.'

'You should,' Jimmy B. agreed brightly, not asking who she was. He wouldn't. None of us ever discussed why we were at the Home. It wasn't an unwritten law, it just never happened. I never knew Jimmy B.'s background or he mine. It was a given. Something had happened and you were in an orphanage. That was it, end of story. Maybe we were simply too wrapped up in ourselves to listen to others. All Jimmy B. knew was that there was a Mrs K. who had something to do with me and she was an adult and no doubt deserved abusing. That was the extent of his knowledge. I never told him of the cruelty she had inflicted upon me and he kept quiet about his own pain. It was the same with the staff. No one came up to you and said, 'Been reading about you and Mrs K. Do you want to talk about it?' The staff and the Home provided shelter and food and warmth. We were looked after well on that score. As for our pain, our loss, they were the lands few ever visited. Instead, people like Jimmy and I concentrated on the present, on the affairs of the day such as stealing and smoking and avoiding being caught.

'Give you a good rollicking, did he?'

'Yeah.' I now changed the subject. 'Where's the rest?'

'Don't know. I think Graham and Terry are upstairs and Big Tommy's gone into town.'

We were not old enough to be allowed out on our own. One of the consequences of this rule was that town, which was just a high street with shops on either side, attained a real mythical quality for all of us. To go into town, on your own – now that was a real treat.

'What time is it?' I asked. 'I think it's twelve.'

I handed back the cigarette. 'Lunch soon. Got any mints?' They were to clean our breath with.

'Nah,' Jimmy said, blue, tantalising smoke issuing from his mouth. The boiler room was cramped, but it was warm. If it hadn't been so dirty it would have been the perfect hangout spot.

'I know who has got some.' 'Who?' Jimmy asked.

I laughed out loud. 'Barry. Fucking smelled them when he was breathing all over me.'

I saw Jimmy's grin widen. 'He does that, doesn't he? Puts his face right up to you when he's going off.' Jimmy chuckled. 'That's what you should have done. Asked him for a mint. Imagine it – "Eh, Barry, after this bollocking is finished I'm going out for a quick fag. Got any mints you can give me so the staff can't smell my breath?"'

We both laughed loudly and then stopped ourselves short in case a staff member went walking by. You were only allowed to be in the boiler room last thing at night. During the day, it was out of bounds.

'Here,' Jimmy said in a much softer voice, 'you're going to the same school as me, aren't you? St Dunstans.'

Jimmy had a rough face, already lined. His mousy hair fell over his creased forehead. His body was stocky, bulky. Jimmy was Irish, Jimmy was a Catholic.

'Yeah, I start next week.'

'Do you want to know something?' 'Yeah.'

Jimmy handed me back the fag. It was right down to the butt now. I squeezed my lips and sucked hard on it only to extract a rough charge of filter smoke. 'What you should do is, you know your knuckles? Hit them against a wall. That's what I do. I bang them against brick walls. It makes them bigger and then when you get in a fight at school you'll win easy. Like this.' Jimmy turned and punched the wall behind him. He showed me his hand.

'Look at my knuckles. Look at how big they are.' He pointed them out admiringly. One of the knuckles was now grazed, a pale red scarring the skin.

'That's through doing that. Punching walls. Tell you, when you hit someone with them, they feel it.'

'Okay then, I'll do it,' I agreed. Jimmy's action had slightly unnerved me but also fascinated me.

'Have you got another fag?' I asked him. 'Nah, run out.'

'What we going to do this afternoon?' 'Don't know. We'll find something.'

And that's why I liked the gang. Without them, you always knew what was going to happen next. With them, you didn't.

The routine for all of us looked after kids had been devised by Barry and Julie. On schooldays you rose at seven in the morning. During the holidays it was eight. Most of us went to bed at nine during the week and ten at weekends.

When you came home from school, you and your fifteen other fellow comrades went straight to the cloakroom, hung up your coats and settled down to polish your shoes. You then placed them in an open wooden locker which had your name on it. (Of course, every night the gang would mix up the shoes, putting brown with black, small with big.) You changed out of your school uniform and into your play clothes. Then you came downstairs for tea. On Fridays, for some reason, you had to press your school trousers. You never did on any other night. After tea sandwiches of jam or marmite or sandwich spread and a cup of tea and a small cake – two of you cleared the table. Two others did the washing and wiping up whilst the rest were free to play in the garden or do homework in the empty dining room.

At about eight thirty, a member of staff would take you and a few others of your age upstairs to wash and change into pyjamas and dressing gowns. Then you came down and sat in the back room with Barry who would normally lie in front of the TV, puffing on his Weights cigarettes.

Julie, a diminutive woman, would sit and sew and Maggie Paterson, unable to criticise us any more as we were now sitting there in full view of her superiors, would make do with a series of barbed comments about English television.

'I dinnae know what's so funny,' she would say as we watched and laughed at the *Morecambe and Wise Show*, 'load of rubbish to me.' Even Barry would raise his eyebrows in despair when he heard such ill-tempered comments.

The programmes other kids mark their childhood with, *Blue Peter*, *Grange Hill*, etc., we missed because they were always on at our teatime. We entered the TV world after we had eaten, completed our chores, washed and changed and had said we had finished our homework.

All the kids would then gravitate towards the small sitting room to lose themselves in the small screen that sat in the left-hand corner of the room. I much preferred music and reading to TV but sometimes such pleasures were impossible in the Home. You couldn't play the record player after a certain time and the staff encouraged us to gather and watch the TV. That way we were all in view. It wasn't that reading books was frowned upon but finding some space and quiet even in a house as big as ours was sometimes difficult. Like noisy jack-in-the-boxes, kids were always popping up in the most unlikely places.

At some point, Barry would enter the room and assume his favourite position, lying down in front of the box with his matches, his small grey ashtray and his packet of Weights ciggies invitingly placed around him. So many times I would fantasise about leaning over and saying, 'Give us a fag, Barry,' and then sparking up.

The rest of us kids gathered around him, sitting on the sofas and chairs or joining him cross-legged on the carpet. The choice of programme, such as it was in those days, was usually decided on a loose vote. This normally worked most nights unless Belinda was in one of her moods. That was when democracy went out of the window, that's when we were forcefully reminded of the hierarchy within the Home.

Belinda lived like one of us. She rose with us, she ate with us, she went on trips with us. But she possessed something we didn't – she had parents: Barry and Julie. What's more, she wasn't afraid to remind us of that fact. It was the main weapon in her armoury.

Therefore, Belinda was not one of us. She was separate. We never drew her in or reached out to her as we would to each other. She belonged to the adults' team. Around Belinda, we kept our mouths carefully shut for fear of treachery and we kept our distance.

To their credit, Barry and Julie did make attempts not to show any favouritism towards her, keen not to upset the balance of the house. But their approach rarely worked. For as she grew older, Belinda learnt what her mother knew already: to exercise power fruitfully one may give with one hand but always threaten to take away with the other. That way, approval will always be sought. Belinda gave her love to her mother but she played havoc with her father's affections. Absolute havoc.

Four of us, Steve, David, Andrew and myself, are sitting watching television. Belinda has just walked in and changed channels.

'Belinda, I was watching that!' 'So what? I want to watch this.' 'But we were all watching it.' 'Don't care.'

David gets up, stomps over to the TV and changes back to the programme we were watching. Belinda sits where her father lies. She leans forward and snaps the switch back. She wears her long blonde hair in two long ponytails that float down her back. I often wonder what she would look like if I were to cut both these strands of hair.

'Belinda!' David shouts in an exasperated tone. 'Don't care. I want to watch this.'

It is the weather forecast.

'Right, I'm going to tell on you,' David shouts.

'Go on then,' Belinda says, not even bothering to turn round. 'Tell my mum or my dad.'

Silence descends. She has invoked the words that leave us powerless. But only for a minute.

'Okay, I will.' David rises and leaves the room. Belinda keeps watching the screen. The man keeps saying it is going to rain.

Half a minute later, Barry walks into the room and Belinda turns to him straight away. 'Dad, I want to watch this but the others won't let me. Anyway, Mummy said I could watch what I wanted.'

'Come on, you lot,' Barry says, smiling falsely at us all, trying to avoid a scene, 'there's nothing you want to watch, is there?'

'I was watching something and Belinda turned it over,' David retorts angrily.

'Yeah, but I am sure it is finished now. Give someone else a turn. Okay? Okay, everyone? Good.' Before David can reply, Barry quickly leaves the room.

'Cow,' David spits out at Belinda's back. We automatically turn to look at him. To swear at Belinda is like swearing in front of staff. Outrageous.

Belinda doesn't do a thing. She sits and watches the commercials. Then she stands and as she walks straight out of the room she says, 'I am going to tell my mum you called me that.'

David doesn't bother to look at her. In fact, he doesn't even bother to turn back the channel. He sits in the glare of the TV, red infusing his freckled cheeks, scarring his face and soul.

It was only much later on that I realised what a curious life Belinda had found herself in. Yes, she had parents but what other child would have to share them and her home with a million other kids?

At nine, you were told to go to bed. You could not get away with just one goodnight. You had to say goodnight to every member of staff present, otherwise they really got offended if you missed them out. So it was, 'Night, Barry. Night.' 'Night, Julie. Night.' 'Night, Pat. Night.'

Up the stairs now and into bed. If you wanted to talk or even fight and play, you would get someone to keep an eye on the crack of the bedroom door for any lurking staff. Occasionally, one of the kids would get out of bed, run over and smack you round the head with a pillow before retreating back to their bed in a fit of the giggles. I never retaliated. These kids were seven, eight years old. I was too big for them.

But you had to be careful. One of Maggie Paterson's favourite tricks was to loiter outside the room, listening in until the moment she chose to suddenly dash into the room, turn on the light and scream, 'Got you now!' She'd tell whoever the offender was to get out of bed. Then she'd smack them on the back of their legs. 'Now stop messing around and get into bed and if I catch you messing around again – my God, I wouldn't want to be in your shoes. Do ye hear me?'

To be honest, I rarely spoke or played around at nights. Most nights I simply went to sleep, only to wake up every morning to Maggie Paterson's unpleasant face and mean mouth: the start of another day in the Home.

I was sat in the garden, I was sat on the small bank that led up to the holly hedge and I was screaming out for a fag. Severe nicotine withdrawal was the result of having little pocket money. Mine was one shilling a week, given to me on a Saturday morning and usually spent on five Park Drive cigarettes by the afternoon. Jimmy, Graham and Terry came down the slope and greeted me with nods and grunts. Graham and Terry made for a funny pair. Graham, slim and always turned out as best he could given the circumstances, and Terry, an overweight, menacing character wearing the same clothes every day. Terry, I was scared of. I just knew he didn't trust or like me and that he was capable of turning on me without warning or reason. When we talked he kept his beady eyes on me for just a second too long – unnerving behaviour and he knew it. They sat down next to me and Terry absent-mindedly dug his foot into the ground and started kicking up small clouds of dirt.

'Got any fags?' he asked. I wished I had so I could please him. I really wanted to say, 'Sure,' and pass him one of the white sticks. But I couldn't.

'Fuck it, then.'

He rustled in his dirty jeans pocket and he brought out a box of matches.

'Watch,' he said.

Terry took out a match, struck it against the side of the matchbox and just as it flared up he brought the match quickly to his mouth and inhaled. He held the smoke in his lungs for a second or so and then he blew it out again.

'Ain't as good as fags,' he said, 'but it's better than nothing.' Graham sat next to him, smiling.

'You try it,' Terry said to me.

I took the box, lit the match and then quickly inhaled the sulphurous smoke. Then I blew it out. It worked. I was cured. No longer would I fear the agony of no nicotine circulating in my body and brain. All I needed was a penny box of matches. Terry, you're a genius. And we smoked the whole matchbox.

It was only later on in life that I discovered that the inhalation of sulphur smoke was responsible for a significant amount of deaths amongst soldiers in the First World War. When firing guns, they inhaled the smoke and about a year later started dropping dead one by one by one.

Jimmy turned to me and said, 'Your name, I can't pronounce it. You got any other names?'

'I've got loads. Paolo, Alberto, Pietro...'

'Alberto. Bert. That's what I'll call you. Bert. It's easier, see?' New home, new name. I was getting kind of used to it.

In the course of settling into my new surroundings, there was so much happening around me, so much to take in, that I had little time for myself. I could still feel the traces of the black cloud in my mind and I knew damn well that life from now on would be rough. But balanced against that was the feeling that I was embarking upon an adventure, the kind you read about in books. Where it would end I didn't know but I imagined it as a story about a child beating all the odds. That was the extent of my plans because otherwise, when I thought about my future, nothing came to mind. When I was at the K.s' I had seen myself in universities and pinstripe suits and bowler hats. Now that had been taken away from me, my life was simply a matter of waking up every day and seeing

where it would take me. There was no future for me any more.
Just the Now.

Part of the wariness we felt for Barry stemmed from his
unpredictable moods. Sometimes he came down the stairs in
the morning cheerily singing. Sometimes you could crack a
cheeky joke and he'd laugh right along with you. Other times
he appeared with a face of thunder and then you avoided him.
If there was one thing guaranteed to cheer him up it was the
sight of a good-looking woman. He couldn't keep his eyes off
them or stop talking about them. If he treated you to a trip
with him when he drove into town, he would always have
one eye trained on the pavement to catch 'a pretty flamingo,'
as he put it.

'Look at that one,' he would shout and invariably he
would sound his horn. If she turned to see what the noise
was he would laugh uproariously. When an attractive woman
appeared on TV, he would pass admiring comments.

'Look at her,' he would say about some actress like
Caroline Munro in a rum advert, 'she's absolutely gorgeous.'
Then he would turn to someone like me or Jimmy and say,
'Isn't that right, boys?' and we would have to nod our heads
and say, 'Yes, Barry.'

What I found strange was that his wife, Julie, didn't seem
to mind his leering at all. She never reprimanded him. If
anything, she was far more concerned about attacking him
for his smoking than anything else. 'It's a disgusting habit
and you shouldn't do it in front of the children,' she would
snap at her husband, normally in the evening when we had
gathered to watch television. The implication was clear: the
kids won't smoke if you don't. But Barry would just groan
and then laugh and ignore her request. 'Bloody kids drive
me to it, don't you?' he would say to the assembled room as
he pulled on another Weights cigarette and filled the small

room with smoke that the likes of myself and Jimmy B. would try and secretly sniff at. Barry drank heavily but this he kept hidden from us. It was only later, when he died of a broken liver, that I realised the extent of his drinking.

Julie's closest friend was Maggie Paterson and not one kid liked Maggie Paterson. She had a terrible temper, a mean disposition. But we liked Mrs Mould, the housekeeper, and we liked Mrs Willoughby, the cook, who had just been divorced. Bronwen Carter, who slept in the upstairs girls' bedroom and just fell short of being really cute, told me on my arrival that the cook had recently reverted to the name Willoughby, her real one, following the split from her husband.

'When she was married guess what her name became?' Bronwen asked.

Bronwen was fourteen or fifteen, but I didn't want to see this girl's knickers, like I did Sandra's. 'What was she called?'

'Mrs Whore. They were Mr and Mrs Whore!'

And Bronwen laughed and I laughed and Bronwen laughed again. She told me this on my first day at the Home. It was only later, when Brownen had long disappeared into the walls of the Home's memory and I got to know what prostitution was about, that I got the joke.

There was a bicycle at the Home, donated by somebody, or maybe left behind by one of the kids – who knows, who cared? All I knew was that to become part of the gang you had to mount the bicycle by the back door. You would then push forward and start pedalling down the drive, achieving within twenty seconds a furious speed which would take you across the main drive, over the garden slope and then up into the air before landing in the garden from a height of about ten feet. The twist was that it wasn't just undertaking this mission that gained you the vital points. The twist was that you were not allowed to fall off the bicycle when you landed. For to fall was to fail and you would have to take the breakneck journey again.

Big Tommy went first, he always did. He was the leader. He sat on that bike, hair pressed back by the wind, and hurtled down towards the garden. We ran behind and heard him shout out as the bike lifted up and sailed into the garden. He came back up the drive, flushed, puffing with success. He was so much more of a man than I could ever hope to be. He stopped, considered all of us who stood in front of him and then he handed the bike to me. He said, 'Your turn.'

Big Tommy had spoken. He must be obeyed. Simple as that. I had no time for nerves or to consider the butterflies in my stomach. Instead, I got on the bike and I pushed off. Before I knew it, I too was hurtling down the sloping drive, gaining more and more pace, the world flashing by me horribly. The trees on either side of me were now a green blur and then I was in the air and just for that second, that second alone, did I understand what it was to be free, to be above human. I closed my eyes but before I had time to pray I landed with a great jolt and the bike jumped up and down along the grass. I gripped hard on its handlebars and magically the bike just bumped along the grass before finally settling. I turned it round, exultant – and there they were, my friends, grinning at me. I looked at them all, flushed with pleasure at my achievement, and saw that even Terry was smiling. With one action I had killed his suspicion of me. I felt exhilarated to have convinced him of my place in the scheme of things. Of my role in the gang. Of course, not a word was spoken between us. No one said, 'You are now with us. You are now one of us.' That's because in the Home actions always spoke louder than anything else.

Jimmy B. and I began school. We would leave after breakfast (usually cereal, bacon and tomatoes) and on the way there we would punch brick walls. I was in the last year of primary school. I had vague notions that I would pass my 11 plus and go to Grammar School.

At school, a Mr Wyatt was my form teacher and he also took us for games. Several nuns also taught there. To my horror, I struggled at school. I found in lessons that I was not as bright as I thought I was. Worse, I let myself down on the football field. I had naturally assumed that I would be picked for the football team but the school had a great team. They had won trophies and cups. I was lucky to make substitute. And I hated that. George Best was never a substitute. Never. It burned me to watch from the sidelines as the team won again and again.

One day, after football practice, as we were trooping off the pitch, one of the kids said, 'Sir, Bert says he lives in an orphanage.'

Mr Wyatt moved quickly to protect me. 'No, it's not an orphanage,' he stated, 'it's a hotel. Bert's parents are away and he's just waiting for them to return. Aren't you, Bert?'

'No, sir,' I replied, eager to explain. 'It's an orphanage. I live in an orphanage.'

'But really it's a hotel,' Mr Wyatt said, encouraging me to follow his line of thought. 'Your parents are abroad and you're waiting for them to come home. Aren't you?'

I could see now what he was doing but it didn't sit right with me. 'No, sir, it's an orphanage. I haven't got any real parents.'

Later, as we all got changed in the dressing rooms, I realised that I was enjoying being the odd one out, the one on the outside, the kid who didn't have parents to wait at the gate for him. It made me feel special, it gave me a certain status. I didn't want to join in. It was too obvious, too easy to have a normal existence. I didn't want that. I wanted to stay on the outside, looking in and feeling apart, feeling exclusive. It felt right for me and it has done ever since. No left-right, left-right, and a nine-to-five for me, whatever the cost.

One day Mothy came to stay. He came to the Home for his holidays because the rest of his life was spent at a special school. Mothy struggled with even the most basic of subjects. He could hardly read or write. But what he lacked in brain power his body more than compensated for. He was a big, muscular boy. Irish, with strong arms. Although his brain failed him at school, he was sharp enough to know his power. He felt strong enough to refuse the gang and that was a major sin.

On his first day at the Home, we offered him the bike test. He refused it and thus he refused us. Big Tommy wasn't happy. Not at all. He was rattled by this defiance. One afternoon, directly after tea, he came into the playroom where I was reading and he said, 'Bert, Mothy says you're an ugly bastard.' I knew immediately that my leader was lying and I knew immediately what my leader required.

I stood up, stood to attention. 'Where is he?'

'In the garden. I'll get the others. You wait outside.'

I went out the back door and waited for my gang. It was cold. Stars were forming above me. I breathed out air from my mouth as if it was smoke. I didn't want to wait around. It would give my nerves the chance to gather and fool with me. I had found that the less you think, the easier it is to enter danger. The gang arrived.

'Bert's going to beat up Mothy,' Tommy announced. 'About fucking time,' Terry, the fat one, grumbled.

'Come on, he's in the garden,' Big Tommy said. We all started down the drive that we raced the bike on. When Mothy saw us come down the slope and into the garden he didn't need telling what was going on in our minds. Over to the right of the garden there were steps leading back up to the house. Mothy ran to them and started to scramble his way to the top. Big Tommy shouted, 'Go to the back door, he'll try and get in there.' He couldn't go through the front door because kids were not allowed to use it. We would dirty the hallway. We had to use the back door where we had to take off our shoes and leave them clean in the cloakroom. Mothy would have to go back round the side of the house to reach the rear entrance. We darted back up the slope, up the side drive, and sure enough there was Mothy coming round the corner making for the back door. He lunged for the handle of the door, opened it and I arrived just in time to push him forward. He went sprawling onto the floor. I dived on top of him and started throwing punches at his head. He immediately pushed himself upwards and I fell off. I scrambled to my feet, as did he, but instead of trying to make it to the door on my right that led to the playroom and safety, he went the other way, towards the toilets and sinks at the back of the cloakroom. A mistake. He was trapped. There was nothing in front of him but us six.

I said, 'Right.'

I marched towards him and I swung a punch that caught him square on the ear. He bent down over the sink and covered his head with his arms. I began pummelling him with my fists. I went mainly for his head and I did so until I was totally exhausted. When I finally stopped, Mothy remained in his protected, curled position, refusing to look at me or the others.

'Don't you ever say that about me again,' I shouted, 'I'll kill you next time.' I was exhilarated; I felt a triumphant wildness pumping in my blood. But as I walked away, Mothy, his head still tucked under his arms, peered out and briefly smiled at me, and it was a smile, like a wild dog baring its teeth, that truly frightened me.

On Tuesday evenings we were allowed to go to a youth club. 'But home by eight thirty,' Barry growled. Most of the time we never attended the club. Instead, we visited the local football club. The team had a small stadium with floodlights. For me, football-mad me, this was glamour. To sit in the stands and watch fast-paced football under an artificial light was absolutely enthralling for me. It was another dimension to lose myself in.

One night, returning from a game, Big Tommy noticed an old 'for sale' board discarded on the ground. He picked it up and with a shout ran over to the railway bridge the rest of us were on and pitched it onto the lines beneath. A huge spark of electricity shot up, volleyed towards us with a loud bang. I had never heard such a noise. It was terrifying. I thought it would wake up the town, which was a mile away. For a second, we stood there transfixed and then we scarpered. I didn't stop running until I reached the cloakroom.

I was first in, fat Terry was the last. We sat in the room, not saying anything, just breathing hard. Just as we were recovering, Maggie Paterson unexpectedly walked in and scrutinised us with her horrible, tiny eyes. 'What are you all so red-faced for?' she demanded in a shrill, Scottish accent. 'Eh? I want to know, like.'

'We had a race home,' Jimmy B. quickly replied. Smart boy, Jimmy. I was getting closer and closer to him. Because of him, I had started realising that intelligence wasn't just about reading books and writing essays and passing exams, as my life up until then had taught me. It was also about cunning and survival. And Jimmy was full of those qualities.

Maggie Paterson viewed us, as she always did, with absolute suspicion and then said, 'Well, take your shoes off and get to bed the lot of you.' She knew something was up but she also knew that tonight would bring her no answer. Instead, she would wait for us to commit some tiny misdemeanour and then she would come down heavily on us to make up for all the crimes she was unaware of.

We trooped upstairs. I went to my room where I undressed and slipped into bed. A boy called David slept in the bed next to me. I stayed awake waiting for him to ask what that terrible bang had been. I stayed awake nervously, expecting the sound of Barry's heavy feet on the stairs and his voice screaming for us to all come down and explain what the hell we had been up to. I lay there waiting for a police car to slide up the drive and to be told that trains had been derailed, people killed or injured. But there was nothing. I waited for an hour and then slipped into sleep.

In the morning, on the way to school, Jimmy B. said, 'You mustn't tell anyone at school or in the Home.' He said it as if I was a rookie who didn't know the ropes. I got slightly annoyed.

'Of course I won't,' I replied testily.

'Barry will go mad. We'll probably get expelled or something.'

'Yeah, I know. Oi! Got any fags?'

'Get your own,' he said. And we walked the rest of the way to school in silence.

A boy called Sean Carrigy was in my class and at the age of ten he was famous. Sean boxed for a local boys' club. None of us boxed. We played football. Already, he was apart from us. What's more, one week the local paper actually ran a photo of Sean fighting. All of us were amazed: Sean Carrigy in a newspaper. Adults were in the papers, not ten-year-old boys. Every time I looked at him I felt disbelief at his achievements. Of course, Sean walked around school like the champion he was and, of course, no one bothered him. He was Sean the boxer. He was in the paper. Sean was tough.

One afternoon at swimming lessons, after our teacher had temporarily left us alone, Sean Carrigy, in front of the whole class, picked up the jumper I had taken off and threw it in the pool. I watched it float upon the blue water, mortified by the terrible knowledge that there was absolutely no way that I could not respond to this flagrant challenge.

'You and me – after school,' I announced and the second the last word tumbled out of my mouth I regretted being alive.

It was the biggest crowd of the season. Everyone was there except Jimmy B., who had stayed at the Home through illness. I was glad of that. I didn't want him to see me beaten up. Everybody else, all the girls and all the boys from the school, it seemed, were there to watch Sean Carrigy destroy Poor Low Hewitt.

'I'm going to smash you in,' Carrigy said to me as we walked around the corner where everyone waited. I agreed with him. I had no reason to believe otherwise. The kids created a space for us and finally the moment was upon me. Sean stood in front of me and raised his fists and I, without even thinking about it, rushed him. I grabbed him round the neck, pulled him down and started punching his head. He pulled away from under my arm and as he did I realised that I hadn't been hurt, that if I didn't box him but wrestled him, I could actually win. That idea – that I could win – momentarily stunned me and the next thing Carrigy had hit my cheek with a punch. But I didn't fall over. I just pushed him up against a fence and he pushed me back. All around us the kids screamed and screamed and screamed. They had expected a slaughter and now they had a fight on their hands. I grabbed Sean's neck again and we fell into a deadlock, him attempting to pull away from me as I held on with all I had.

The next thing I knew there was a shout and Mr Wyatt was pushing his way through the kids who were now scattering every which way.

'You two – stop it now. I said, stop it!' I let go of Sean immediately.

'Both of you will see me tomorrow,' he shouted. 'Now, go home.'

I did. I walked home alone and I walked home so relieved that I hadn't been beaten bloody. And all because I had somehow found the nous to wrestle and not box. When I got home I found Jimmy B. in his bedroom and I said to him, 'You know what, I think I'll stop punching walls from now on.'

I got nothing more than a bollocking for the fight, and I was used to them by now. Thankfully, the Home wasn't informed. Sean and I were shouted at for five minutes or so and then we left Mr Wyatt's office – but I did so as a tough guy. My status in the playground was enormous now. I had taken on Sean Carrigy – Sean Carrigy! – and not been beaten bloody. And so it was that I never had another fight at school for four years, simply because the word on me was that I was a tough nut. Hard to beat. One to avoid. And Sean Carrigy and I never spoke to each other ever again.

One day I came home from school and Big Tommy was gone. Disappeared. No longer in care. Out in the world now. Out of my life as well. No farewell, nothing. Just gone, taken off the map of our world. Barry told me, 'He's going to join the army.' That was it. I was saddened. So were the rest of the gang. Without a leader, it wouldn't be long before we splintered in two. I think we knew that then.

Life kept cheating me. I should have learnt not to rely on anybody. John and Molly Brown, Big Tommy, they all looked out for themselves. They had left me and they didn't care. So why should I? But still, I retained a faith in people that totally outweighed my experience of them. I think it's because 'looked after kids' fall into two categories: we are either absolute bastards or we are saints. We either want to avenge the world or we want to save it. I was in the latter category. I wanted to help people. I did so because I wanted to be liked. If I saw anyone upset it got to me, got to me bad. Kids at school thought of me as tough but that was just through luck and hanging out with the right people. The truth was that I was beginning to get scared. The gang wasn't as important without Tommy and I was starting to lose interest in maintaining my tough boy act. Blankets of doubt started to form in my mind, dark and heavy. On the way home from school, walking alone on cold winter evenings, I began to ask myself how my life had happened? A year ago I was a public schoolboy. Now I was an orphan in a children's home. I had no parents, no money, no life. Everything my friends had, I was denied – clothes, records and freedom. All I had was the gang and that didn't seem enough any more.

I don't know if it was Big Tommy's departure that sparked it but not long afterwards Barry and Julie called me into the sitting room. They told me that they were extremely fond of me. They told me not to worry, and that they would always be at the Home until I had finished my exams and gone to university. They would treat me like their own son, they promised. I half believed them and I half didn't care. The father I wanted was John Brown. Not Barry. Barry couldn't talk to me about cricket. He was Welsh, he liked rugby. I hated rugby. I wasn't particularly bothered about Julie either. She seemed okay but she didn't match up to Molly. But Barry and Julie wanted to treat me like a son. So what could I do except walk away feeling a little bit more special than any of the other kids in the Home? Of course, I never told Jimmy B. about this. He would have just laughed at me for believing such rubbish. As for Terry and Graham, they would have beaten me up for being a favoured son.

All three of the gang would go away during school holidays. They went to stay briefly with what family they could muster between them. For this half-term holiday, I was left alone with the younger kids. The first morning, I was in the playroom when I heard the front door open.

'Take your bag upstairs and then come down and see me,' I heard Barry say. I went back to the football annual I was reading. It was four years out of date. Five minutes later, I looked up and Mothy was standing there.

'Ain't got your friends with you now, have you?' he jeered.

His fists were closed tight and as he advanced upon me he broke into that smile, the one he had given me in the cloakroom the night I beat him up. I didn't realise until he was upon me and furiously piling his fists into my face that it was the smile of pure revenge.

It's strange to admire someone whose sport you care nothing for but I love it when Bob Hewitt, the tennis player, appears on TV. His appearance, however brief, allows me to spin off inside my mind to far, far better places. When Bob is mentioned or when he appears on the small screen, I smile inside. For it means I can start the film in my head, the one in which I discover that Bob and I are related.

The picture opens on a sunny morning. I am sitting in the Home's sitting room. In front of me is a newspaper. I glance at it and there it is, front cover: BOB HEWITT FINDS SON. He's been living abroad all these years, getting famous, getting rich and now he has discovered me. He is my father... maybe my brother...actually, I don't care. He is a Hewitt and he is coming to rescue me. That's what counts.

I put down the paper and look out of the window and a white Rolls Royce comes purring up the drive. This gracious

car comes to a slow, gracious halt. I pick up the small suitcase
standing next to me and walk outside. A smiling chauffeur
wearing a grey suit and a grey cap emerges and says 'Hello.'
He clicks his fingers and smiles. The back door magically
opens. I clamber into the luxurious darkness and settle down
on cool, leather seats. The door shuts softly. The driver gets
in, smiles at me again and turns the wheel.

Suddenly I am standing in a large garden. The weather
is glorious and the air is still, peaceful. There is lemonade on
the table and a blue sky above me. There are people standing
around and they laugh and they smile, and then Bob, bald
but with small kind eyes, emerges from the group and puts a
large comforting arm around my shoulder. 'This is your home
now,' he says, 'and this,' he says, nodding back to the smiling
expectant faces behind him, 'is your family.'

A brilliant warmth moves through me. I lean into Bob's
body and smile. Life from now on will be warm, it will be safe.

Seven

The Road Long and Winding

The fever that assailed me after the robbery finally vanished from my body. I woke up after two weeks away and my world had changed again. I was brought tomato soup and toast in bed and told that I had wandered close to my end. Very close. Still, I was on the mend and, what's more, things had started to tilt my way. The school had been in touch. I wouldn't be expelled. I was to be given one more chance. Furthermore, there would be no charges pressed by the police. I was too young, they said. So was Laz. 'Just know we are watching you,' was the message from the local boys in blue.

The best news was when David, who slept in the bed next to me, popped in later and said, 'Maggie Paterson is leaving. She's got another job.' That aided my recovery, of that I have no doubt. Within a week I was up and about. I was also trying hard to avoid the boiler room. The time had come to quit smoking. For good. That was it. I'd learnt my lesson. Not another fag. Ever. They had put my health in real danger. No more, no more. On the down side, I had to retrieve the money in the boiler room for the man with the kids who we had so cruelly robbed and I would also be grounded for a month. No going out, restricted to the grounds.

Barry and Julie queued up to sit on my bed and tell me again and again, wasn't I a lucky boy not to have gone to court? Wasn't I a lucky boy not to have gone to court? I dutifully nodded my head, although at this point in my life I didn't feel lucky at all. I was just relieved to be alive and anxious, anxious to get back to school and football and music and my friends. But I had to agree with them about one thing: no more cigarettes. The little brown-and-white rockets had nearly killed me. They weren't going to get another chance. As the song says, I might be afraid of living but I'm far too scared to die.

Jimmy B. handed me his fag – we were having one between us – and said, 'Leaving tomorrow. Going to another place.'

I blew out the smoke from my lungs.

'Shit,' I said. I was hurt by the revelation but had no way of expressing it. And so we stood the rest of the fag in silence. Both of us, alone again, naturally.

At school, I played it quiet. To some, I was a hero for my endeavours. To the teachers, I was a marked boy. So I played it quiet. Kept my head down. Had to. They had sent the big boys in.

My file dated April 1970. The social worker writes, 'I have talked at some length with Paola, [!] about staeling [sic]; told him that he is likely to be at least given a very severe reprimand by a high-ranking police officer but really is in danger of appearing before a court. The headmaster put Paola on Cond. Discharge. When he knew about the recent stealing, the head gave Paola the cane. Paola does not appear to resent this; he simply told me that the head would have caned him before but he, Paola, was not well. It would seem that at the moment Paola is not showing any signs of repentance. Although after I had finished talking with him, Paola was seen to be in tears. Whether this was because I had suggested that his savings may have to be used to put back the money he had stolen, I am not sure.'

In an earlier file the same social worker wonders about my intelligence. To him, my brain-power is a complete puzzle. He notes that I have been tested many times but the result is always the same: bright boy, ahead of his years in language and literacy but in other subjects, maths and science particularly, forget about it. But in his own fields, yes – a bright boy. Yet, the social worker continues in a slightly baffled tone, my personal experience of him is somewhat different. For example, he states, 'I tell him things time and time again, specifically about his mother and two sisters, and he seems totally unable to grasp the plot. He will ask me questions that I have already told him the answers to.'

I know what he means. Sometimes I asked such questions deliberately just to break the awkward silence between us as we sat facing each other in the sitting room. But I also recall that dimness which often suffused my mind whenever talk arose about my circumstances or my crushed life. I would much rather think about football or music or clothes than what the hell had happened and why. Plus, I had nothing to say to this particular man. I didn't feel any kinship with him and so wasn't going to open up for him. He was stiff and boring. Didn't like anything I liked. Didn't, in fact, seem to like anything.

Within five minutes of his arrival at the Home we were sat down and he was sipping tea and smiling. I was a million miles away.

The truth is, my mind had no time for anything that was not designed to fire my imagination or which spoke of my past. It is the same now. Cars, how they work? No interest. Shelves, how they are fixed? No interest. Gardens, how they flourish? No interest. People told me about such things but I paid them no mind. If their words didn't touch on books or football or music or clothes, my brain would simply turn down the volume of their words and drift away to another world. By the time I came back to earth the person talking would be slightly exasperated. They would think me a lemon. They would think me unable to grasp things. Which was absolutely fine. I wouldn't show them the real me. In fact, I couldn't show them the real me. I had no idea who he was. That's why I was building my own secretive world. So one day I could meet me there. That was the mission, the unstated dream, a trait I shared with all of the kids in that Home. We all built dreams that allowed us to escape. The girls dreamt of rich, handsome men whisking them away to marriage and luxury and devotion and the boys dreamt of inheriting huge riches and becoming famous.

At night, in the stillness of the dark and with the warm light of the moon upon us, all of us looked after kids, the boys and the girls, reached upwards to much better worlds.

* * *

In 1970 and again in '71, I was shocked to discover that the world was not solid. All of us have to face up to this frightening truth at some point in our lives. It came to me during these two years. Up until then the world had been many things to me: evil, terrifying, ugly, nasty, occasionally beautiful – but it had always been solid. There were things in it that I just knew would never die, that would always be there to make the world a Forever place. I was wrong.

In 1970 The Beatles split up and in 1971 Muhammad Ali lost to Joe Frazier. Both disasters still invoke reverberations of trauma inside me to this day. I had clung so hard to them. I couldn't believe that the radio would no longer play new Lennon and McCartney music. Throughout my whole childhood, they had been as permanent as air. They had thrilled me with their magic, aroused me with their words, captivated me with their sound and above all given me a strange kind of hope, especially when they sang about taking sad songs and making them better. Now they were gone and the little radios that seemed to follow me into every house I lived in would never be quite as magical again. Because of this, the world felt a little less than it had been before.

As for Muhammad Ali, he remained, still standing, still unbeaten, still making solid the universe. I wasn't there at the time but at some point in the early '60s Ali picked up his shadow and flung it across the entire world. It meant that, whether you knew it or not, we all lived and breathed and grew up in its magic.

In 1967 they stopped him from boxing but they couldn't stop him reaching us. He was always with us. It didn't matter if he was fighting or not. He was there, on the radio, on the TV, shouting and joking and hollering for the righteous – all of us with a certain kind of soul and heart cheering him on like no other. Ali was all of us. Three years later he was boxing again, once again rousing families from their beds to gather round the radio in the early hours of the morning to will him on to victory. For when Ali won, so did the world.

In 1971 he fought Joe Frazier for his title; his rightful title as heavyweight champion of the world. I will always remember the shock of disappointment that howled through me like raw electricity the day I rushed downstairs to find out he had lost to Frazier. It took minutes to absorb the terrible news. First, I thought of him hurt and injured. Then for the very first time in my life I thought the impossible: I thought of him knocked down and helpless. The terrible image took my breath away and frightened me. I quickly threw it away, that terrible image.

Then I worried for him. I worried for Ali like I worried about all things close to my heart. How would he be able to face the world and explain his defeat after all the boasts and the predictions that he had made? What would he say? How would he say it? How could he evade the taunts of the non-believers now? It was as if the enemy had won. They hadn't, but the '60s died that day. Right was no longer invincible over wrong and real magic had begun to leave the world, slowly and surely disappearing into the air.

I switched off the radio which carried this tragic story and I walked away to school, trying to adapt to a world that had suddenly become very fragile. I felt lost. Absolutely lost, for if you could not believe in Ali, who could you believe in? It was only much later in life that I discovered the answer to that question. Ali had told us it all along but I had been too slow to see the true meaning behind his words – which was: believe first and foremost in yourself. Do that and all else then follows, like rivers flowing into the sea, guarded as always by the floating butterfly and the sting of the bee.

* * *

During this time I had stayed in contact with just one person from my past: Mrs K.'s mother, Ida Foulis. I hadn't seen much of her during my last two or three years at the hands of Mrs K. and that, as I would later find out, was because they had violently disagreed over Elizabeth's upbringing. Infuriated by her criticisms, the cruel daughter had banished her mother to the wasteland where she put all people who dared question her authority. Ida found me and she wrote to Barry and requested I come and stay with her down in Hove. It was the start of irregular visits to her which I thoroughly enjoyed. Her flat was warm, big and homely. Better still, I could do what I liked. She let me smoke in front of her and she gave me double my usual pocket money. She let me come and go as I pleased. I could stay in bed late in the morning, go to it late at night. The only thing we never spoke about was her daughter. I never asked and she never told. Both of us knew we were far better off without her.

On my reluctant Sunday afternoons, she would put me on the train home. When I arrived in town I would then have to call Barry for him to come and pick me up.

On my second visit to Ida, I returned home to find the phones near the station trashed. They had been involved in their regular Saturday-night high-street punch-up with the locals and were now dangling uselessly, their broken arms swinging above a bed of shattered glass. I decided to walk towards the Home and find another. Halfway there, I found an unscathed red box, stepped in, placed my unopened packet of Embassy on the shelf beside the phone and fiddled in my trousers for change. Just then, I heard a car horn behind me. I swivelled and saw Barry pulling up to the box. He smiled at me. I smiled back and then his face turned absolutely sour. He had spotted my cigs on the iron shelf.

We drive back to the Home alone in silence. When we get in, Barry marches into every room and calls all the children and all the staff to the hallway. He waits impatiently as everyone gathers around in a circle, expectant and worried but curious.

'All here,' he finally says. He then pulls me to the centre of the circle and places me in front of him. He pulls out my packet of cigarettes from his pocket and he says, 'I found these cigarettes on this boy today. We had been generous and given him a weekend leave and he came home with these. Despite being told a million times that cigarettes will kill him, still he carries on.'

Barry's voice is harsh, edgy.

'Do you know what that makes him? Do you? I'll tell you. Stupid, absolutely stupid.'

Barry now crumples the packet up in his hand and goes over to the red dog bowl that sits in its normal position against the dining-room wall. He kneels down and starts crumpling the contents of the packet into the bowl.

'Do you know what it also makes him?' he says, turning to address his startled audience. 'Do you know what he reminds me of?' He doesn't wait for an answer. 'A dog!' he screams. 'That is what he is like for cigarettes. A dog. A slave. Look!' Barry now starts sniffing the bowl in which brown lumps of baccy lie uselessly.

'He's a dog!' he shouts again, 'A dog who gets a sniff of tobacco and can't help himself. He would rather smoke it and kill himself. He nearly did recently and still he carries on.'

I'm standing there absolutely transfixed by Barry's antics. So is everyone else. Now Barry stands up. Someone moves a switch and his voice goes down a few notches.

'We are not dogs. Paulo is. Paulo is a dog. His craving for cigarettes makes him one. But the rest of you are not. Is that clear?' A nodding of heads all around the hallway.

Satisfied, Barry surveys his troops. He has our full attention and that knowledge pleases him so much. He doesn't want the moment to end.

'If I find any of you kids with fags I will treat you like a dog. You will eat dog food and be treated like a dog for a week. Is that clear? Paulo, you're grounded until I say so. That is your punishment. You can also clean the dog bowl. The rest of you, watch out. Now go back to whatever it was you were doing.'

'Oh good,' Terry whispers from behind me, ''cos I was just in the boiler room having a fag.' Luckily, Barry missed my smile.

* * *

At the Home, we arrived from all points of the universe. We gathered in that small sitting room to watch TV and our roots stretched out to Europe and Africa and America. The group was made up of all ages – from three and four right up to seventeen. There were the dark-haired, the fair-haired, the lumpy and the slim. There were plain faces and ugly faces. There were short and tall. But above all, there was Emily. Fifteen, sandy-haired, slim and breathtakingly beautiful, Emily had been blessed with a body that would draw men to her for years and years to come. All of us fell in love with her, all of us imagined time spent in her arms. The older you were, the more vivid the dream became.

For me, just a kiss, one long, lingering kiss, would have sufficed. That was the extent of my desire. For others, a different story existed. But amongst us there was one guy above all who remained absolutely transfixed by her sassy ways and divine body; one guy who made no effort to disguise his lust. His name was Barry Isleworth.

Holiday time. The Home decamps to the Isle of Wight. We stay in a long hut, filled with rows of beds, for two whole weeks. Like a prisoner of war, I feel listless, bored. The island is boring, so are the trips to the beach where we munch on sandwich-spread sandwiches peppered with sand, where the wind never dies down, where the sun shines briefly, disappears, then re-emerges laughing at us, where the sea is so cold I go nowhere near the water.

'Come on, Paulo,' Barry shouts. 'We're on holiday, enjoy yourself.'

I am sat silent, digging my toes into the beach. Barry sits in brown trunks, on a large towel. 'Look at those legs,' he says, 'best pair of legs in the country. All the girls love them. That's all you need, Paulo. Pair of legs like mine, can't fail.'

His eyes settle on Emily and they widen. She is approaching us in a brown bikini for which her breasts are already too prominent. Water drips from her hair and settles on her thin, brown stomach. Breathtaking.

'Isn't that true, Emily? Great legs I've got.' 'Yes,' she replies. 'Amazing.'

Fifteen and she already has his mark. She will play him like a yo-yo. Up and down, up and down. Barry reaches over to his trousers which lie next to him. They are grey flares and from them he pulls out two shilling pieces.

'You and Paulo, go and get some drinks. Don't tell the others, okay? Hey! And mind you don't spill those cups,' he says, nodding towards her breasts and laughing loudly.

'Oh, I think I'll be able to manage that, Barry. Come on, Paulo. Let's go the café.'

'That's my girl,' he shouts after us.

I walk beside her not daring to look at her slim, tanned body. I fumble for words. At thirteen, you swing on a bridge between childhood and adulthood. Emily's beauty, made glorious by her bikini, smashes that bridge, reduces me to a little boy again. Only a man can gain this woman and I keenly feel that distance between us. Unexpectedly, I find myself asking what she is going to do when she leaves school.

Her reply is direct, memorable. 'Get married to a rich man as soon as possible.'

'Really?'

'Of course. Find myself some rich guy and marry him soon as possible.'

'But that's not love,' I reply meekly. She snorts.

'Look, Paulo, you have to get what you can get. No one is going to give you anything. You're the same. You're stuck here. Do you really think anyone is going to help you? You got any parents?' I shake my head. 'The only way out is to use everybody. Me, I'm going to find a rich man and marry him. That's what I am going to do.'

She says these words with such conviction that to this day, whenever I think of Emily, I imagine her walking through a large house, a sports car purring expectantly on the gravel of a long drive. I also think of that day as one of the last times I felt like such a little boy.

'If you've spilled any, I'll clean it off for you,' Barry shouts lewdly when we get back to the group. Emily smiles gracefully, takes a tantalising sip of her drink then stretches her long, brown body out on a meagre towel, ignoring Barry whose eyes burn into her body. She closes her eyes to the fleeting sun, peaceful in her strength, content in the knowledge that all beautiful women are blessed with: you play it right, you play it cool, and life is yours for the taking.

Julie, meanwhile, sits nearby, corralling kids, giving advice, giving instructions, ignoring her husband's staring and biding her time.

* * *

Back home, Saturday afternoon in town: Graham, Terry and me. When we needed new clothes, the Home gave us pink slips of paper known as order forms. On them, Barry would write out the item needed, sign the form and hand it to us. We would then go to the relevant shops and use them as payment slips. Naturally, this arrangement was not made with the one or two boutiques that were in town, where you could purchase brogues and crombies and Ben Shermans, but with cheap shops such as Curtess Shoes – only three pounds ninety-nine a pair.

We go to a department store on the High Street. Graham wants to look at men's clothes. Not to buy them, just to look. We ask a young suit passing by the lift where to go to. It is his first day on the job.

'I'm really not sure,' he says, turning to look at the signs, 'let me see.' 'Fucking hell,' I say to him, 'you fucking work here and you don't fucking know. What a wanker you are.'

As soon as I've said this, out of the corner of my eye I see what looks like a large fly heading for me. Whack. Graham's leather gloves have whipped my cheeks. They turn red with pain and embarrassment.

'You rude kid. How dare you talk to that man like that. It's not funny,' he half shouts at me. 'Now apologise.'

Now I am confused. Swearing, insulting people, that was part of being in the gang. Surely. That's what I thought it was about. Us against them. Orphans against adults. The Home versus the rest. Not now it isn't. Graham has just humiliated me in public right in front of the enemy.

I spend the rest of the day with them in silence. Neither Graham nor Terry talks to me, which is fine. Jimmy B. is my mate, not them. Jimmy B. understands. They don't. Only thing is, Jimmy B. is gone.

I trusted no one but the gang. In the gang we were all the same, brought down by life but brought together. That's what links me with every other looked after kid, past present and future. And now the gang was splintering. Silently, I hand in my resignation and a week later Colin Nollie arrives.

* * *

Staff members were to be avoided at all costs. When we did encounter them, we played different roles. Subservient to some, cheeky to others, nice to some, nasty to the weak. It all depended on what they allowed you to get away with and how far you could push them. Whether they realised this, I have no idea. But at the Home they certainly discussed us.

These events were called case studies. Every six months, your social worker and someone from the Social Services would come to the Home and sit in the living room with Barry and Julie and a couple of other staff members and discuss your progress. They would drink tea and nibble on biscuits. Then, at some point, Barry would walk over and close the door. The meeting of your meriting would begin.

I would sit next door in the playroom, trying to hear what was being said about me, but the low murmur of their voices never reached me. After five minutes, I would get bored, frustrated and go elsewhere, usually the garden, to kick a ball around or maybe disappear into the small bamboo forest, settle down and just dream away the life that was being discussed at that very moment in time.

And nowadays, if I am out and about and I see anyone, be it on the street or in a shop, a bar, or a public place – and I mean anyone – talking and throwing glances my way, I know without a shadow of a doubt they are discussing me or laughing at me. And it makes me want to hurt them so badly.

In my files, three bulging folders thick, perhaps the most perceptive comment now appears.

'Paolo has his ups and downs in regard to his place in the school football XI. It seems that though he is quite a good player he tends to hang onto the ball too much…it is, I think, just that he is carrying on the same behaviour pattern as when he played for hours with a ball in the back garden and on the field this tends to manifest itself. He seems unable to appreciate the fact that he is only part of the team and shouldn't try and do all the work himself.'

* * *

On Sundays, in the early evenings, I would get myself near the radio in the playroom and settle down. I intended to talk to no one and no one could talk to me. I was there to listen to the chart rundown. This was one of the most vital parts of the week for me. Who was top and who was bottom in this week's hit parade was a matter of enormous importance. It somehow defined the week ahead. Would the tune I was hoping for reach number one or would some sappy number steal it away? If 'Chirpy Chirpy Cheep Cheep' was number one again, or if 'Knock Three Times' by Dawn reigned supreme, then it felt like a massive blow against me and all the bands I loved. On the other hand, if 'Double Barrel' by Dave and Ansel Collins or 'Hot Love' by T. Rex had made it, it was like winning at football, that same exhilaration.

Pop music dominated my life. I listened to it as much as I could. I read about it and I memorised it. I drank greedily from its well because, compared to my former life, I now had so much more access to it.

The result of this increased exposure was that Marc Bolan became my hero. It wasn't his looks that got me – too glittery, too silly – nor was it his clothes. It was the music; those guitars and those strange lyrics which suggested the existence of another universe altogether. 'Telegram Sam, I'm your main-man...'; 'Get it on, bang a gong...'; 'Well, you're my woman of gold and you're not very old, ah uh...'

We weren't allowed to put up posters on the Home's bedroom wall that I shared with five others – 'Well, if you put one up everyone else will and then where will we be?' was Maggie Paterson's explanation – but I read everything I could about him. I committed to memory his lyrics from Disc 45, my favourite magazine, and I stared at photos of him for hours. I found it remarkable that this strangely dressed man with his strangely worded songs could be screamed at by girls but equally adored by boys such as myself. It made me conceive of the pop world as a remarkable place where all of us were equal, where all of us were brought together as one through music.

Yet my admiration for Marc had to remain a secret in some quarters and dare not reveal itself. For not everyone dug Marc and those who didn't were the boys at school who considered themselves bright, intelligent, a cut above the likes of Laz and Vic and Enzo and Pete, boys who frightened them with their lack of ambition, their pissing around at the back of the class, their suedehead clothes and their cheeky remarks.

For this select crowd who boasted of taking eight or nine O levels, music was the line that established your intelligence.

For them, pop music reflected my friends: it was too cheap, too vulgar. For them, Yes, Emerson, Lake and Palmer, progressive music and your ability to understand it separated you from the crowd, put you a cut above. Only those who could listen to an album of this stuff for hours and hours had something worthwhile going for them. Their favourite put-down about anyone when they were sure no one was listening in was this: 'He likes chart music,' snigger, snigger.

My trouble was that I liked both. I loved Marc Bolan and I liked this new singer, Rod Stewart. But I also liked some of the stuff these other guys brought in to school like Led Zeppelin or Deep Purple, even some of the lesser known stuff like early Pink Floyd or The Groundhogs or this mad jazz guy called Dick Heckstall-Smith. But from these people, I kept Marc a secret. If his name came up, I kept silent. I betrayed him because I wanted to belong. I wanted to be in with the smart kids as well as the other guys. I needed to be seen as bright as well as loveable. I wanted to be respected for my intelligence. But I also wanted to wear the clothes and walk the walk of the glamour kids who didn't care about exams or school, who were not dependent on anything the adult world said was good. I hovered between both groups and the result was that I stayed outside of both of them.

Looked after kids have a million questions but never quite believe the answers when they are given. That's because our lives are so removed from others' that everything becomes a half-dream.

* * *

Colin beamed down into the Home just as Christmas was approaching. For several weeks, as all good friends do, we circled each other. He was a tall, slim boy with a shock of hair that Barry constantly moaned about. It was light-coloured and grew like an Afro. Every day, Barry told him to cut it. Every day, Colin agreed to and walked away. Underneath it, his face always seemed set in a slightly mocking smile. It was an expression that I would get to know very well later on in life when I sat in rooms where marijuana smoke hung like a blanket. People thought he was displaying contempt when they saw him nodding his head and inwardly smiling. I didn't. I thought he existed on another level.

Certainly, he was the first to introduce me to hippie culture. He played me the Woodstock album relentlessly. He spoke of how he was going to travel the world. He especially wanted to see India. He wanted to go to festivals and take acid. He often spoke about Jimi Hendrix and, when no one was looking, he wore beads around his neck. Like all of us '70s kids, his timing was ten years out. He was born to live in the '60s but had had the misfortune to arrive too late. By the time he was ready, the '60s were gone. Everyone had gone home. The crowd, the band and the road-crew. Teenage living in the '70s was merely about picking up what they had left behind in the empty stadiums.

Like many hippies, Colin came from a rich background. Every week at the Home, without fail, brown parcels would arrive for him, sent by his Turkish father. Inside, there would be clothes and records and envelopes with money inside them. When we finally acknowledged each other and got to chatting I found not only a close ally but an inexhaustible supply of tobacco. It was wonderful never having to worry where my next smoke was coming from. Colin was kind and generous towards me and not just with cigs.

One day in the garden, as we sat cautiously smoking, he told me not to worry about Barry's outbursts. 'You shouldn't get upset by him,' he urged. 'When he shouts at me and has those fits, I think of him as a mental patient. I think he's really funny.'

'What?' Naturally, Colin knew nothing of my mother. 'When he shouts and screams, he is really funny.'

'What, you laugh at him?' In no way did I believe anyone laughed at Barry. Not even the charismatic Colin.

'Not at him,' he replied, 'I don't stand there laughing out loud, but I think of him as a clown. Next time he has you up, don't get afraid. That's what he wants. Try and stand back and watch him. He's so funny. The way he shouts and screams, I piss myself.'

We heard a voice at the top of the garden stairs – Esther's, I think it was – shouting, 'Dinner's ready.'

We stubbed out our fags and made our way to the dining room. It was half-term and so most of the other kids were there. But Colin only shared his knowledge with me.

* * *

At Christmas, parcels of clothes and presents would arrive at the Home, donated by charity shops or concerned individuals. These would be handed out on Christmas Day along with presents from the staff, bought out of the Home's funds. These tended to be really boring items such as socks or hairbrushes. You never got a Faces album or a book on The Beatles. You never got a present to talk about at school in cold January classes.

The only good thing about Christmas was that on the day itself all children were excused their duties. The staff did all the work. You got the day off. In the morning we gathered by the tree to receive our presents. That morning, the talk in the bedroom as we got dressed hurriedly had been about who was getting that year's special present. This was an extra gift given to a child specially selected by Barry and Julie. This year, it was obviously a bicycle that one of us was to be blessed with. My heart quickened when I saw it parked next to the Christmas tree. Tinsel had been placed on its wrapped bars. I looked at it and knew it was mine. I thought this for two reasons; I had been at the Home for two years now and I had never received the prize. And also I was Barry and Julie's favourite. They had told me twice now that I was like a son to them.

'We'll be with you until you go to university,' Barry had said. 'Promise.' Every Christmas, Barry and Julie handed out the presents. This year we sat, as usual, in a circle and chucked the wrapping paper into the middle of the floor.

'And now,' Julie finally announced, 'time for the special present...'

I got ready to stand and then I heard Stephen D.'s name called out instead. I have never forgotten that gut-wrenching feeling which tears into you when anticipation is obliterated by the world outside, and, what's more, obliterated by your own doing.

* * *

Colin and I were stood in the boiler room smoking when Barry suddenly shouted down the stairs, 'Right, you two — get up here. Now.'

He took us into the playroom and he began his raging. As he did, Colin nudged my arm and I recalled his advice. We spent the whole afternoon together, acting out Barry going mad at us and laughing until I thought I would split in two. I loved Colin from that wonderful day on.

Except that Colin couldn't fight and so I never told him about the beatings that Mothy was still giving me. I didn't tell anyone. I endured them and then I walked away, head throbbing, body aching, eyes watering. I had no defence against him. I was too weak to fight and too scared to talk. He often told me that if I ever told anyone about these beatings he would kill me. But I had no one to tell. If I went to Barry or a staff member I would be safe for a while. But I couldn't be protected all the time. That was impossible. At some point he would make his move, and when Mothy came to take his revenge…well, I couldn't even think of that scenario without my soul freezing over in fright.

I was getting to a desperate level when, all of sudden, he was gone. He had been transferred to another home, no doubt to make another child's life a misery. Suddenly, I was free. No more beatings, no more worrying about where he was or what was to come.

Of course, I still woke up apprehensive, worried about all kinds of things, but my major concern had been lifted. As the days progressed without him, I began to relax a little. Not a lot but a little. It showed. At school, I came top in English. Mrs Gardiner told me as I was going home one night.

'You did very well in your essay,' she said. 'You must be proud.' I shrugged my shoulders, showed her little joy. I have never been good at accepting compliments. The book we had been studying was *A Tale of Two Cities* by Charles Dickens. I loved his work and his stories. I could quote from them verbatim. Plus, I had read this one when I was ten.

I also came second in history and fourth in geography. Other subjects I coped with. I still hadn't spoke to She but I had heard from one of her friends that she liked me and this thrilled me to my heart. That news and Mothy vanishing from my life was more than enough to convince me that maybe there was some good to be gleaned from life. Maybe.

At the Home, life was a lot easier without Maggie Paterson on my back. I played my records, I read my books. I hung out with Colin and I smoked cigs and my football skills developed.

I started to think that the darkness was finally lifting.

And then Colin was gone. His father called him and he went. Gone. In a puff of his smoke.

* * *

Three years after meeting her for the very first time in my life, I went to see my mother again. I was taken by my new social worker, who I liked. She was tall, American and measured. She was new to the game and told me so. Don't expect miracles, she said, and I admired her honesty. After a couple of visits, she started arranging for my mother and me to meet. It was April when we drove off on a cold afternoon to the hospital my mother lived and worked in. When the journey began, our talk was chatty, good-natured. By the time we were close to the hospital and my social worker was peering left and right and saying in a matter-of-fact tone, 'Should be around here somewhere…' I was quiet. Very quiet. A minute later I looked up to my right and there it was – a huge red-brick building sat on the top of a hill. It looked much bigger than the Home, far more imposing.

'Up there,' I said, pointing.

We turned into the long, winding drive that took us to the hospital's front door. As we made our way up in the car, my social worker started saying things to try and keep the situation normal. ('Bit bendy, this road, eh, Paulo?' that kind of thing.) But all I could hear was the voice in my head saying, 'You shouldn't be here, you shouldn't be here. Mother or not, you shouldn't be here.'

At reception, we were told to wait for a Miss Benkins. We sat for five minutes, my social worker throwing in the odd comment ('Um, well, that's a nice vase of flowers over there') and me nodding my head and swallowing nerves.

A small, compact woman, hair tightly pulled back, glasses balanced on her nose, now appeared. This was Miss Benkins. 'Come to my office,' she said briskly. We stood and followed her. The office was cramped. It contained a desk covered by files, paper, pens and a file holder; above it on the wall was a huge map of the area along with a fire emergency notice and a clock.

She nodded for us to sit on the two chairs facing her. She began by welcoming us to the hospital. She said that my mother was stable and in good spirits. There was nothing to report as such. My mother was a good patient. She had been working in the glass factory but now she had switched to the laundry. She seemed to like it better there. That jarred me for a second. Surely making glass was less tiring than dealing with mounds of bed linen?

Then Miss Benkins clasped her hands together and said to me, 'One bit of advice, if I may, it would be better in your conversation with her not to mention your father. She does tend to get very upset when he is mentioned.'

My father. Straight away my mind conjured up a tall, dark-haired, craggy-faced man. I thought of him amidst Canadian forests and mountains and rivers. I saw him fishing in a hat and him turning to smile at me. I saw a wooden hut and a fire. From a distance, I saw him and I skimming stones across a large pond. I saw him laughing with me and throwing his arm around my neck. Father and son.

'Okay,' Miss Benkins said, interrupting my film. 'If you follow me I'll show you where to go,' she said, leading us out of the office. 'If you go to the end of this corridor, turn left and follow the corridor all the way down to the bottom you will come to a dining room where your mother will be waiting for you. It's been lovely meeting you. Any problems, there will be a staff member nearby.'

We said farewell and walked as directed, turning left onto a corridor that sloped downwards. In the distance, I heard a noise. When we came around the first bend, I saw what was causing it.

There were six of them, four on one side, two on the other, five men and one woman. They were standing against the wall, dressed in shabby dressing gowns and thin, striped pyjamas. They were talking to themselves, their voices meshing together as a cloud of babble and moans. None of them took any notice of us. As we passed by they simply carried on talking to themselves. Some of them remained still, others had the shakes, their heads uncontrollably snapping back, mouths dripping with saliva, their arms flailing uselessly in the air. The one I glanced at had eyes rolling. He snorted, sniffled. His body shook. He seemed to be in conversation with something or someone.

These were my mother's fellow patients. The people she shared her home with. I kept my head bowed down but couldn't help looking at them, fascinated and repulsed in equal measure by their violent inner disturbances. All the time, I feared that one might reach out to grab me as they would in a nightmare but none did. They stood in their favourite spots and they raged against their distraught private worlds.

At the end of this corridor, its walls swaying with the sounds of the demented, we saw the dining room and I caught a glimpse of my mother. She had on a dark-blue cardigan, a light-blue stripy T-shirt, a grey skirt and dainty shoes. She wore make-up and perfume and she was putting a cigarette into her lips, sucking on it, leaving lipstick traces on its brown top. Her hair was greyer than I recalled and she looked sad and reflective but as soon as she saw me, she stood and cried, 'Hello, Paul, hello. Hello.'

I was glad to see her.

My social worker writes of that day, 'Conversation flowed smoothly enough with both she and Paulo enquiring about news regarding each other. She took us to her cottage where we chatted in the sitting room. Both stated that they would like to see each other again in July when Paulo begins his summer holiday.'

* * *

On arriving at school, Enzo Esposito would stand in front of a mirror applying lacquer to the back of his hair which he would then part, carefully pushing the now stiffened hair round the sides of his neck and under his shirt. School rules commanded that no pupil's hair should lie upon their shirt collar. Punishment was to visit the barber's within a day. Enzo had been caught three times now and, as far as he was concerned, enough was enough – hence the lacquer and subtle brushing which made his hair look as short as anyone else's.

'Let's see Jock Cosgrave, the wanker, get me now,' he sneers. Four of us are sitting watching him as Pete Garland walks in. 'Wotcha.'

'Wotcha.'

'Oi, Bones, give us an advert,' Enzo demands. He has finished with his hair and is now admiring his strong Neapolitan looks in the mirror.

Pete puts down his sandwich-box and says in a note-perfect voice, 'Fresh every day, the Sunblest way...'

'Give us another,' I say.

Pete turned to me. 'You could use a cruise with P&O...'

'What about...'

The doors swing open again. Tommy, Vic and Laz walk in, looking like a gang, a proper gang.

'Oi, who wants to see our marks?' Vic says, a huge smile on his face.

The three of them have just been to Cosgrave. This morning, they were caught smoking on the golf course.

'What did he give you?' I ask.

'Four strokes each,' Tommy proudly informs me. 'Come on then,' says Laz. 'Into the bog.'

We all crowd into the boys' toilet.

'Me first,' Laz says. He drops his trousers and pants and then bends over slightly.

'Anything there?' he asks.

I see four deep, red lines that have slashed his white skin.

'Fucking hell,' Pete says.

'Good, ain't they?' Laz says. He stands, pulling up his clothes. Everyone laughs. But not me. Suddenly, I am back at Mrs K.'s, bent over a table about to be caned.

'What about me?' Vic says, almost pleading.

'Here,' Tommy says as Vic bends over, 'fancy going to the flicks? *Kelly's Heroes* is on. It's not an X, so we can bunk it in. Who fancies going?'

There's a chorus of yeah, yeahs all around me. 'When you going?' I ask, still staring into nothing. 'Saturday afternoon.'

I could manage that one. 'Yeah. I'll come,' I say. 'See ya there.'

And then I walk out of the cloakroom and find my way to the playing field outside. I walk onto it and survey the houses dotted in the distance. Were there other Mrs K.'s out there right now, beating the young, taking their revenge? I doubted it. I imagine ordinary lives, ordinary people. I imagine my life in such a house and as I do the image of Laz's scarred skin rears up in my head again. I turn away. I see a group of boys playing football in the playground. I run to them. They're first-year kids.

'Oi,' I say, 'give us a game.' (I tell a lie. I didn't say it, I demanded it.) 'Sure,' says the boy quickly. 'You're on our side.'

Saturday afternoon and the ABC is empty of my friends. I can't see them anywhere. I walk up and down but can't find them. They must be coming to the next show, I figure. Unless of course they were never coming in the first place and this is a wind-up. I look for a seat. This is my first time at this cinema, although I have been to the Odeon up by the station to see *Lord of the Flies* with the school. We sat in the balcony and Vic flicked sweet papers on the heads below him whilst everyone else chatted, which annoyed me. I wanted to watch that film.

I slide into a seat and I pull out my brown-and-white bullets. Cinemas are great for smoking in. It's dark and no one bothers you. I fumble for matches. Shit, I haven't got any. I look around the mainly deserted cinema. Where are my friends? A guy right at the end of my row is waving a box of Swan Vestas matches at me. He waves them again. I stand up and go and sit next to him. He pushes the flame towards me and I catch a light. I settle back. He says something but I don't know what. He has greasy, swept-back hair, is middle-aged and there is something about him that feels slightly dirty. I don't like him but I feel obliged to sit next to him.

He says something again. I ignore him. He says it again. I sit forward, away from him. He says it again. I look back. He has released his penis and he is jerking it hard. All the time, he had been saying to me, 'Look.' Immediately, I stand up and move away. So does he. He quickly walks up the middle aisle and I walk to the end of my row, turn left and go to the box office in the carpeted empty hallway.

A girl sits motionless and bored behind her till. 'Excuse me, miss, there's someone just been wanking in there – I mean, masturbating.'

She looks blankly at me. Then she slides off her stool and nearly disappears under the counter. She comes out from behind the till and goes straight into the manager's office. He appears about ten seconds later.

That night the police arrive at the Home. They have already called Barry so he knows everything. They take me into the empty dining room and they open up a book full of photos. On the first page, I see him straight away. His name is Skilton.

'Yeah, thought so,' one of the policemen says. His voice sounds tired, disinterested. Then he snaps shut the book.

Three weeks later, I am in court. Barry and my social worker have taken me. I feel great. I have the morning off school which means I miss double maths and geography. The trial will finish at eleven thirty so I can then saunter into school just in time for lunch. Better still – and what I'm really excited about – is that in the afternoon we play Highlands at football, a team we rarely lose to. It's not often a day like this falls into my lap.

As we wait for the proceedings to start, I sit at a table and read *The Times* newspaper cover to cover. Policemen stand in clusters of blue around me.

'Look at him,' Barry says, 'cool as a cucumber. A bloody Perry Mason, this boy.'

A court clerk approaches Barry and they and my social worker talk in low voices. I carry on reading. Then the clerk moves away and Barry taps me on the shoulder.

'Okay, Paulo, might as well go home. They've postponed the hearing to this afternoon.'

I can't believe it. It's not fair. I'm going to miss the game. Bloody hell and shit. I wish I had kept my gob shut now and not said a word at the cinema. I start praying that this thing will be over in time for kick-off. It's all I can think about. Back in court in the afternoon, I sit and stare at the clock. It moves faster than ever. By the time it is three o'clock, I am resigned to missing the game.

Much to my extreme indifference, Skilton is found guilty, fined twenty pounds and told he mustn't do anything like it again for at least two years. Something like that. I was beyond caring. All I could think about was the game at school. In fact, I spent the whole afternoon imagining and playing it.

We won 5–0 and I got a hat-trick. But I never got Skilton's leering face out of my mind for years.

* * *

I wake up in a world that God has forgotten to colour. Everything, from the sky downwards, seems to be grey, seems to be neutral. It is summertime in Britain and the Home is on holiday. Again.

I have snapped to life in a hut on the Isle of Wight. Strangely, it is early. I normally try to sleep, staff members allowing, at least ten hours. Not today. Around me, in bunk beds, about twenty kids and teenagers sleep, their warm dreams escaping from their mouths and fading into the dull morning light. I find myself staring at the back of Martin's mousy hair, tangled up and true in the bunk bed next to me. It's no coincidence that we sleep near each other. At the Home, he and I share a bedroom together and we are close. We are mates. He is a small compact boy, muscular in body and cheeky in nature. Most of the staff call him as lazy as sin but I like his determination to go his own way in life. It's a trait we share.

Martin has honest eyes and an open nature. You know exactly where you stand with him. You never smell deceit or slyness upon him unless, of course, he is in trouble with someone. It is a rare quality in 'normal' human beings, let alone a young man whose life has been shattered because of someone else's alcohol problem. Of late, we have been arguing a lot about money. He's for it, I'm against. I think there is much more to life than chasing cash. He thinks I'm a fool. What's more, I am the worst kind of fool. I am a fool with a brain.

'What more is there to life?' he demands of me.

'I don't know.'

'There ain't nothing else. Believe me.' 'There's got to be more than just money.' 'Why?'

'Because there has to be.' 'You know your trouble?' 'Yeah, yeah, yeah. What?'

'You listen to those teachers too much. You think reading all those books is going to get you somewhere. It won't.

You'll die poor. You'll die in the gutter with not a penny to your name.'

'I won't.'

'You will if you carry on like you do.'

A thought flashes towards me and I catch it. 'You know what we should do? How we should settle this?'

'How?' he asks.

'Okay. This is what we'll do. When we leave here, you go your way and I go mine. But in twenty years' time – no, better, when we're forty years old – we both have to meet up on a set date and compare our lives. We have to go to a pub, sit down and see who was right and who was wrong.'

'I'll do that with pleasure,' he replies.

'Then we'll sit and see who's got the most and who is the happiest.' 'I'll meet you in my Rolls Royce. It's a date.'

'A date?' I say. 'Oooh, you are awful – but I like you.'

At the end of such arguments, a brief silence will descend upon us and we lie in the dark of the room, contemplating ourselves, contemplating the future to come. Then our minds will inevitably turn to pleasures of a more assured kind.

'Oi, fancy going next door?' Martin asks, expectation high in his voice. When asked the question, I never bother to answer. It's a given that I'll say 'yes.' We rise silently and tiptoe through the boys' room that adjoins ours. Fred, Dave and Steve sleep here. Out on the landing, we make a sharp left and enter the girls' bedroom. There Kim and Emily await us. Kim is Martin's 'Home' girl.

They often disappear at some point during the day. They either go to the boiler room or the bamboo forest and they vigorously explore each other. One night Martin told me that both Kim and Emily were on the pill. 'It's true,' he said, 'she showed them to me.' Someone in charge had decided that it was better for the girls to swallow bitter little pills than conceive babies. For once, someone in charge had made the right decision.

'Kim,' Martin whispers loudly. 'Over here.'

Martin goes to the right, I to the left. Both Emily and I know we are getting crumbs off the table in this arrangement. She certainly hasn't got the hots for me but what the hell. It's never earth-shattering between us but nor is it that much of a disaster. I go to her bed and kneel down beside her. She brushes back her hair and I plunge my lips onto hers. After a short while, I slip my hand down her nightie and rub her breasts like a window cleaner. Round and round and round. We keep kissing. I move my hand off her breasts and push it farther down, towards her mound. She tenses as I try to jam my fingers into her dry circle. Still, we kiss. I push and push with my finger whilst next to me Martin lies on top of Kim, an enviable motion of sighs and grunts and movement.

I take my hand away from Emily's mound and pick up her right arm, guiding it towards my exposed burning centre. She half-heartedly caresses me. I begin to rub her breasts again. The minutes pass. I can't help myself. Now I make my move. I pull back her sheets and go to lie on top of her.

No way. Not that. Emily will go far but not with me. She pulls the sheets back over herself and hisses 'No!' at me. Before I can respond, I hear Martin say something to Kim. He moves off her bed. He taps me on the shoulder and I stand and move away. We creep back through the little boys' room and into our linen sheets and wool blankets.

Silence. After a minute or so, Martin asks, 'Did you shag her?' I say, 'Yeah, of course. What about you?'

'Yeah, twice,' he replies, before turning over and adding, 'Emily says you got a small prick. See ya in the morning, mate.'

I flush with rage. 'What did she say?' I say, half-sitting up in bed. Martin keeps his back to me. 'Sucker,' he says and he laughs. 'Wanker,' I reply, lying down and feeling very relieved.

When I am sure he is fast asleep, I move my hand downwards and bring myself to the place Emily has denied me.

Of course, on holiday we couldn't get anywhere near the girls. At night they slept with all the other girls and the women staff members in one big room. During the day they were under strict supervision as the staff were all on full alert with regards to our safety. It wasn't surprising. The Home was in a strange place. The sea was nearby. Anything could happen with twenty children in such a scenario. Martin and I just had to content ourselves with the knowledge, as Barry kept glancing at them every ten minutes as they lay sunbathing, that only we were allowed that which their bikinis sought to cover.

I turn the other way in bed and look now at Des's face. Des is a part-time member of the Home. During school-time he attends a boarding school somewhere between Nottingham and Sheffield. He and I are close too, although that fact is in no way surprising. Des is consumed by music too. Somehow he attains albums by obscure American groups with names like Steely Dan and The Eagles and we spend hours playing them, Des sitting close, explaining why the songs sound so good and who the musicians are and what their backgrounds are. I sit there and realise with a shudder that Des is exactly the kind of boy I imagined I would be when I was at the K.s' – clever, self-assured, witty, happy and confident. I want to be as accomplished as he is. I want to be as measured as he is in everything he does. And I'm not the only one. Des tells me that a teacher at his school has been pestering him all term to write the school's Christmas play. Des reports this to me in a casual manner and the very next day I march into school and eagerly seek out Mrs Gardiner, our form teacher.

'Miss, can I write a play for the school?'

'Yes,' she says with a surprising enthusiasm, 'that would be lovely.' That morning I feel so special. I will write the school play. By the time the night came, I know I will never write such a thing. I wouldn't know where to begin.

Des plays the guitar. It is the only time he seems vulnerable. He sits there and, as his long fingers move easily up and down the fretboard, the melancholia inside him rises up and shows in his large brown eyes. It's why all the staff like him. He could be an artist, they all say of him. So talented. Like Paul Simon, says one. Not like Gary Glitter, says the other and they laugh. The consensus is that he will go far. Julie says it too. It is noticeable how her conversation of late now includes names such as Steely Dan or The Eagles.

Des isn't snoring right now, just breathing heavily through his nose. I turn away and look up at the ceiling. I hate these holidays. I hate the jolly little voice I have to put on when Barry shouts over to me, 'Having a good holiday, Paulo?' and I have to smile and say, 'Yeah, great,' when all the time I'd rather be at the Home, playing music, sneaking off for fags and trying to talk Emily into following Martin and Kim into the bamboo forest.

'Come on, campers, rise and shine. Wakey, wakey.'

I sit up a little in bed, look to my left. Pete Mac has entered the room. He is Maggie Paterson's replacement, a chunky man with soft, brown eyes and a beard. Martin recently told me that Pete and Barry don't like each other. He heard them briefly arguing over something or other the other week, with Barry finishing the spat by stating, 'Yeah, well, when you're in charge you can do it your way. But until then...'

I'd rather have Pete in charge any day. He's far easier to run rings round.

'Come on, boys, rise and shine.' Eyes click open around me but bodies lie still.

'Come on, we haven't got all day.' Little Fred now sits up in bed. He rubs his eyes, yawns and asks, 'Wot we doing today, Pete?'

'We are going to the beach today. And it is "What are we doing today," not [Pete adopts a rough accent] "Wot we doing today."'

Fred's face creases into a smile and his deep-blue eyes sparkle a little. He will break hearts soon, this boy. He pulls back his sheets and jumps down from his bed and so do I. Underneath me, Andrew the diabetic is lying there with his eyes open, staring at nothing. He looks lost, forlorn. It happens to all of us. On odd days, you wake and straight away you feel scared to your stomach but you have no idea why. It's like someone has sucked the life out of you while you were sleeping. Today, I would have ruffled his hair and told him, 'Come on.' But back then, forget about it. Like all looked after kids, I am far too wrapped up in myself to do anything for him.

I follow little Fred into the bathroom. I splash my face quite a few times and then select my toothbrush from the glass on the ledge. I smear paste on the bristles and fill my mouth with the colours, red and white. Fred does the same. We brush, turning energetically occasionally as in a dance to look at each other. Over to our left is a side door which leads into the girls' bedroom.

The door is half-open and I can hear another staff member, Rosie, telling everyone to get up. Her voice is softer than Pete Mac's.

'Come on, girls, time to rise. It's a lovely day outside.' Then I hear Sarah's voice. 'Why do I have to get up?'

'Because we're on holiday, we're going to the beach,' Rosie explains. 'But if we're on holiday why can't we stay in bed?'

'Because that's not what you do on holiday.' 'Why not?'

'Because it's not,' says Rosie, now a little more sharply. 'Well, why isn't it?'

'Because it isn't.' 'But why isn't it?'

'Sarah Davies, you get out of that bed right now and stop asking such silly questions,' shouts Rosie, 'and do it now.'

Sarah breaks into a long nine-year-old's piercing cry. 'Get those blankets off your head. Get dressed.'

There is a muffled sound of tears and screams. Then a minute's silence.

'Okay,' Rosie firmly says, 'don't get out of bed, stay in there. See if I care.' All the time this is going on the girls have been coming into the bathroom to clean their teeth. They are dressed in long nighties and pyjamas. Some are tutting at Sarah, others are urging her on with their generous smiles. 'I'm going to breakfast,' we hear Rosie say. 'You can stay in bed all day. I don't give a damn.' Then we hear a door shut.

After a minute or so Sarah appears at the doorway, a cheeky grin playing on her lips. One–nil to her, and the day has hardly begun.

I finish my brushing and think about Colin Nollie, who I miss. He once recently told me that the adults who work at the Home, who shepherd us from pillar to post, from childhood to our exit, are just as screwed up as the kids. The hours are long, the pay must be dreadful and the abuse is pretty constant, so what other explanation is there? They were running from themselves or they were on a power trip.

Either way, they were damaged goods as well. 'The house is filled top to bottom with them,' he said with a small laugh. That was his theory, and I remember it well because when he told it smoke was issuing from his nose and I still hadn't worked out how to do that yet with my fag.

'They like being with us because it kind of makes them feel good,' he told me. 'Either they're on a power trip or they think they're Mother Teresa.'

I do miss Colin and his take on the world. He thought differently to others because adults didn't scare him and that left him free to come up with all kinds of angles on them. By making them absurd, he began to free me from my fear of them. I have never forgotten the lesson. He went after only six or seven months at the Home and when he did I felt the same – as frustrated and angry – as when Jimmy B. was beamed away from me. I felt hopeless. I couldn't change things. I just had to stand it. Colin's rich father, who'd settled in Thailand, had finally found a new life and wanted to include him in it. Who cares what Paulo thinks? After all, for several years you are just a bystander in your own life. Other people push it along. You're just in it for the ride. Bye-bye, Colin.

I go back to my bed and change into my favourite clothes: a white cheesecloth shirt, jeans and clogs. I put on my favourite coloured tank top. I walk back into the dining room and see staff and kids dotted around three large tables. Julie looks up at me. She says, 'Paulo, we're going to the beach today. Don't wear your best clothes.'

'Where's Barry?' I hear Stephen ask.

'Probably sleeping it off,' Pete Mac whispers to no one in particular. 'Go on,' Julie urges me, 'go and change. You can wear those clothes when we go to the pantomime later on in the week.' I turn and walk back to my bed and start unbuttoning my cheesecloth shirt. Some material gets snagged in the small crucifix that is tied around my neck and I pull it free. I have no idea why I still wear the thing. I gave up being a Catholic about four months ago and, suitably enough, it was at Christmas that I turned my back on God.

On Christmas Eve, I had been allowed to go to midnight mass for the first time ever. I was taken by a temporary staff member. I think his name was David but I can't be sure – so many people pass before my eyes that I stopped trying to learn all their names a long time ago. No point in getting too friendly. When we arrived at the church, people in overcoats and scarves were spilling out onto the steps. We gently pushed through a wall of cashmere and crombie material and found ourselves a little space by a large stone pillar. We dipped fingers into cold holy water and we crossed ourselves. The mass had started. Paddy Donovan, a good friend from school, sidled over to me. 'Wotcha.'

'Wotcha.'

'You should have been here earlier,' he whispered. 'Why?'

'Billy the Bottle got thrown out.' Billy the Bottle was the town drunk, usually found slumped in a semi-coma up by the train station, where the platform bar was about the only place that he could find service. No one else wanted his money, for Billy the Bottle was banned from every shop in town. He had achieved this unique status a month before when he casually walked into an electrical showroom with a rail porter's trolley he had just stolen. He jammed it under a fridge and started wheeling the machine out onto the street. A shop assistant gave chase. Billy scarpered down the high street but he was drunk and soon lost control of the trolley. The fridge sailed into the window of a betting shop and Billy ran into a passing policeman and got himself arrested.

'He started singing but it wasn't carols,' Paddy whispered. 'He was singing football songs.'

'What team does he support?' I asked Paddy as we both sniggered – although inside of me something didn't sit right. Jesus hugged the drunks and he attacked the money lenders. My church was doing the exact opposite. And at Christmas as well, the time of goodwill to all men.

Very real seeds of doubt were planted in my mind that night, seeds that came to fruition when the time of Lent arrived a few months later. At my school, we always knew when Lent was coming because Mr Deish started getting up at assembly and asked us not to go to the tuck shop that day but to give the money to charity instead. I never bothered with him. I figured, I am that charity. Plus, all my money went on cigarettes, not sweets. I wasn't even sure where the tuck shop was. Yet that year, and I don't know why it happened but it did, something in Deish's sanctimonious speech got to me. As he stood on that stage and dribbled on and on, a plan formulated in my brain. After assembly, I pulled Enzo Esposito aside and told him about it. I proposed that at midday we waited by the assembly hall for the trolley containing the teacher's lunches to be pushed through. We would tell whoever was in charge of that trolley that the teachers were making us take it to the staff room as a punishment. We would then wheel it into our cloakroom. I would deliver a note to the teachers saying that if they wanted their lunch they would have to pay a shilling for every plate. That money would then go to charity. Just like ours did.

I thought it was a brilliant plan, audacious but inspired. I thought the teachers would line up and grudgingly but cheerily admit defeat and hand over their money. They would all say, 'That Paulo Hewitt, he is a cheeky so-and-so but what a great trick he has played on us. Good on him. Bloody good on him. That pupil has taught us a lesson.'

I didn't count on Mr Deish slamming into the cloakroom, face as red as a bull. I didn't count on him screaming and screaming about how hard teachers worked and how they never got any time to themselves and to have their lunch stolen by a couple of stupid boys like us was absolutely outrageous and if he was the headmaster he would expel us this instant. I hadn't counted on any of that. But that's because I didn't realise until that day just how full of hypocrites my church was. They talked the talk, but when it came down to it they were as greedy and as sinful as those they despised. I walked away from the church that day. I dumped it and I forgot about it. That day, I shed its grip on me.

Only you don't forget about it. Catholicism never leaves you. Oh you can sneer and you can complain and never go to mass for the rest of your life but your soul will always live in its shadow. It's because they got you at an early age. They injected that mercury liquid into your bloodstream and they filled your head with their stories and your heart with their fear. They took you to churches where their images of torture and beauty surrounded you and they scared you silly with their rituals and their mysteries, their talk of eternal damnation. They did so because they knew what you didn't: that you can run and run from them but you can never run from yourself. And that is the rock upon which the Catholic church is built.

* * *

I slip off my jeans. They are not Levis and I want a pair so bad, so bad. I have even been thinking of asking certain people to buy me some. First, I thought of Mrs K.'s mother down in

Hove. But her kindness to me was such that I didn't feel right pushing her any further. For some reason, I then thought of asking my mother for help. I had last seen her two months ago. Again, we had walked down that corridor of horrors to find her in the dining room. Again, she had got all dressed up to meet me and my social worker and at first the talk was easy and bouncy. But soon it petered out. So my mother and I sat there, occasionally grinning at each other, both of us lost in our respective worlds. She was slipping into her twilight zone and I was ready to leave and go home, to play the new records which had just been donated by the shop in town.

My social worker did the best she could. She broke the silence often with little chit-chat but it was to no avail. The afternoon was lost. Finally, my mother said, 'I go now.'

As we got ready to leave I remembered my Levis. I went to say something but then I looked at my mother staring into space and nothingness and realised how absolutely stupid I was to even think of asking her for anything.

'Bye-bye, Paul. Bye-bye.'

'Mama?' I said to her, the first time I had ever used that term. 'Si?' she instinctively replied.

'My name is Paulo, not Paul.'

She hesitated for a couple of seconds, surveyed me curiously and then broke into her smile.

'Okay, Paolo, okay. Bye-bye. Bye-bye.'

And she never called me Paul again, even if she had thought that this was what I had wanted all along.

No Levis then. I hated that fact, hated that my life now seemed to be full of nothing more than wanting and desiring but never ever getting. I was nearly sixteen and I was filled with longings that dominated my state of mind. I wanted fashionable clothes, I wanted new records. I wanted a chopper bike with ape-hangers for handles and the gear-stick in front.

I didn't want a space hopper because they were stupid, but I wanted to watch *The Sweeney* every day of my life. I wanted green pound notes in my pocket and I wanted to grow up and be a football commentator, like Brian Moore on *The Big Match*. (Well, I did until I was heard in the bath one evening, commenting on an imaginary Spurs–Chelsea game. When I came out of the bathroom about four of the kids fell about laughing. I was so embarrassed that I dropped the idea instantly.) I wanted to get served in pubs and wear a red suit like Ron Wood on the inside cover of Rod Stewart's album Smiler. I wanted to be a journalist on a music paper. More specifically, I wanted to be a writer on the *New Musical Express*. I wanted to have my picture printed in it every week and write long articles about Rod Stewart. I wanted to smoke twenty Du Maurier cigarettes every day as I hammered away at the typewriter. I wanted to pass all my exams and not worry about my future. I wanted Her to be my girlfriend. In my mind, I came to a stop there because that last wish was now totally unattainable.

The girls in my year had grown up now. Their jumpers pushed out, and a month was now more than just a passage of time. The girls in my year had a sophistication about them now and that was why they didn't date boys of the same age. They didn't have to. Now they were whisked off to country pubs by eighteen-year-old men who worked and earned money and bought them Babychams and snowballs all night long. Some even drove cars – like the guy She was now rumoured to be seeing. What chance did any of us have against such opposition?

How was I to know then that beauty at an early age is an utter curse for so many girls? At fifteen, they are already in tune with life and fabulously in tune with themselves. All the stupidity that boys their age display has somehow dropped away. They are true glamour, true beauty and they are only interested in men who have three or four years on them.

But it's a wrong turn. These men court them and woo them and flatter them and make them feel so wanted that at eighteen, the girls marry them. By twenty-one, it's all over. Their looks are fading and their days are spent pushing a pram around town, living in a council house, living with baby's screams and regretting the day they said yes to their husband who now works long hours, comes home pissed every night, carries a beer belly and has the nerve to lust after their younger sister during roast beef Sunday lunches at the family home. These erstwhile roses now look in the mirror and they no longer see what made them so special and it breaks their hearts.

It was the girls who were lucky enough to flower later on in life, were ignored by the Cortina Chaps and were able to soar a little bit higher.

I pull on my shorts quickly, as I always do. To be honest, I prefer to change alone or in the dark. I am happiest that way. My nightmare is having to unrobe in the school changing-room. Everyone seems much bigger than me. Two boys in particular have been blessed with things a mile and a half long. They stand in the shower for what seems like hours, their appendages dangling free. I look at them with sly fascination and I ask myself, if he's a virgin, is it more shameful to be one when your thing is that big?

The other week I was trying hard not to stare at Pete Russell's when I overheard two of my teammates talking about going out that night.

One of them, Giuseppe, said to his close mate, Sam, 'You coming out tonight?' and Sam replied, 'Nah, I've only got enough money for nine pints.' Most of my friends are drinking now. On Friday nights, they go to the pub opposite the local disco where the landlord is lax in who he chooses to serve. Unfortunately, his generosity doesn't extend to me and my mate Vic. Each time we have entered the pub he has laughed us out of it. His laughter is not surprising. Our heads just about reach the bar. But last week we triumphed. As usual, I met Vic by the bus stop but instead of trying the same pub again, he sprang a surprise.

'Come on, we'll try The Crown on this side of the road. There's too many in that other place.' We wandered up the street and tentatively pushed open the pub door. The pub was half-empty but everyone in there turned to look at us. A dark, wooden bar was directly in front of us and from behind it, the landlord, a middle-aged man with a belly to match his years, looked at us with a smile. Here we go again, I thought. 'What can I do for you, lads?' he said as we stopped in front of him.

'Two light and bitters, please,' Vic replied, his voice as easy as they come.

The landlord shook his head and laughed. 'Come on, boys, you're not even fifteen are ya?'

'Yeah, we are,' Vic said defensively.

A drunk, who I had noticed slumped at the end of the bar, suddenly lifted his head.

'Oi, Dave,' he cried, 'give them a drink, fuck's sake.'

The landlord turned to him. 'Bill, it's out of the question. Look at them.'

'Give 'em a drink. They got to start sometime.' 'It's out of the question.'

'Dave, let me ask you something. How old were you when you had your first drink, uh? Tell me, how old were ya?'

'That doesn't...'

'Uh-uh,' he said, interrupting, 'how old? Come on, tell us.' The barman looked back at our expectant faces.

'Come on, Dave,' exhorted the drunk, 'tell the world.'

'Jesus Christ,' the barman said. 'Okay, two light and bitters but that's it.' He poured the drinks and placed them down in front of us.

'Four and six, and you drink them over in that corner there.' We picked up the drinks and saluted the drunk at the end. He waved back at us and then slumped back onto the bar, lost in the darkness.

* * *

Having changed, I fold up my best clothes and leave them on the bed and I walk back into the dining room and Julie looks up at me. 'That's better, Paulo.' They still can't get my name right.

Belinda, her daughter, sits opposite her, studiously ignoring everyone. Des is sitting next to Julie, munching on toast. He is smiling in agreement with Julie. For the first time I sense something odd.

'There's cereal over there,' Julie says, nodding over to the long table. She is a small woman, whose shoulders are slightly hunched. Her hair is parted in the middle and has been given a '60s-type flourish as it drops down either side of her cheeks. Today she is wearing a tight white T-shirt, black shorts and denim sandals. Her eyes remain cool but deceptive. This is a woman who takes in everything going on around her. She is Mother. She runs the Home now – not Barry, it's Julie. Barry shouts and screams and makes his presence felt but it's all bluff. Julie runs him and she runs the Home and she does so by exerting a tight control over all of us.

Her way is to gather favourites around her and grant their wishes – yes, Paulo, you have pleased me with your willingness to do my bidding and your interest in what I have to say, so yes, you can stay out a bit longer even if it is a school night. And yes, Des, you can have those clogs and plectrums for your guitar. But no, Martin, you can't go there or do that because you refuse to play the game. Give and hold, give and hold. Last year she took me to see Godspell at a theatre in London. It was a real treat catching the train to London and walking wide-eyed through millions of Londoners. A real treat. That night I was the favoured one and I would have done anything for Julie had she asked. Except, it would seem, to say thank you – for the next day, in a fit of pique, she put me on double work duties for a week and I was told I was the most selfish boy in the world. 'I take you out on a treat and you can't even say thank you. What kind of a boy are you?' This didn't bother me. Of course I was selfish. Every looked after kid is. You don't have your life shattered forever and then not spend most of the time thinking about it and yourself. It's only when you meet others worse off that you give a little.

I sit down opposite Martin and begin eating. Milk marks my mouth. 'Are there any newspapers around?' I ask him.

'They don't have them on the island,' he replies.

I look at him momentarily. Then he grins and says, 'Sucker.' 'Morning, Barry,' I hear David Westbrook say on the table behind me.

His words are followed by a low murmur of greetings from the kids and staff. I look around to see Barry slowly heading towards the cereal table. He doesn't say a word or acknowledge anyone. He simply slouches into the room wearing shorts and flip-flops and a lemon-coloured short-sleeved shirt. The collar is not a button-down one and so is of no interest to me. He passes Julie's table but he doesn't acknowledge her either. Des keeps his head down. I don't blame him. Barry's eyes are red and there is a ray of pain that is splitting his forehead in two. Anything could trigger off a rage from him. Barry pours himself some cereal and then he goes and sits with Val and Roger, the posh brother and sister who joined the Home about three months ago. They look embarrassed to be the ones he has elected to sit with, embarrassed and not a little worried. But Barry pays them no attention. He just sits at their table, going snap, crackle and pop, like his life is about to go.

Down at the beach the wind whips off the sea and straight into my shaking wet body. I sit with a towel hanging uselessly round my neck, my feet digging into the sand for some kind of warmth. In front of me, Fred and Esther build tiny sandcastles and Mary then runs over and kicks them in the air. Pete Mac is lying in shallow water with Martin and a couple of other kids, doling out swimming lessons. Emily and Kim are a bit further out, treading water and watching the men in trunks walking past. Once in a while they laugh uproariously. Meanwhile, alone at the water's edge, about half a mile to the right, Barry looks out to sea and sits alone. Belinda his daughter is playing nearby.

I am sitting with Val and Roger and some other kids as well as with Rosemary, the hippie staff member. Sometimes she comes into work wearing cheesecloth shirts, jeans and clogs except for today where she sports a brown bikini with light-brown stripes running through it. To my surprise her breasts are enormous and so I am hovering close by, sneaking glances, getting ideas.

'Oh my God,' she says suddenly. 'Where's Bugsy?'

Bugsy is half-Chinese and is the youngest and smallest of the group. When he smiles, hearts crack. Rosemary's head turns this way and that, desperately looking for him. He's not there. She stands up. 'Bugsy,' she cries, 'Bugsy.' Worry and terror are mixed up in her voice.

I see Peter Mac look up from where he is in the shallow waters to see what is happening. Barry glances over.

'Bugsy! Bugsy!'

'He's over there,' Roger says, pointing behind her.

Indeed he is – only you can't see his body. All you can see is his small head popping up from the sand. He is smiling like crazy. Next to him, his undertaker, Gary, sits with a sand-smeared spade in his hand, smiling beautifully as well. He has made him into a sandcastle.

'Oh my God,' Rosemary says as she cools down. 'Oh my God.' Meanwhile, her full breasts wobble deliciously.

Bored, I stand up and say to Rosemary, 'I'm going to look at some postcards.'

'Fine.' She has her eyes on Bugsy. I am the least of her problems. I trudge through the sand to the shop by the beach's entrance where they sell sweets, ice cream, cigarettes, newspapers, cups of coffee and tea. The shop is called The Happy Swimmer. As I approach it, I case the joint and realise that if I had fags and matches on me right now I could nip behind the shop, light up and be totally out of view from everyone. Outside the shop there are three large swivel-racks jammed with postcards. I stop in front of one and look mainly at the saucy cards. Some of the girls depicted in them remind me of Rosemary. As I'm looking, the swivel-rack unexpectedly turns. I realise that there is someone behind it looking at cards. In fact, there are two people, for I can hear their voices which, for some reason, they are keeping very low. I stand absolutely still and listen in amusement.

'He knows.' 'He doesn't.'

'He does. I can tell.' 'Has he said anything?'

'No, but I have been with him for eight years now. I know when he knows.'

'Why, has this happened before?'

'No, of course not. Don't be so stupid.' 'Do you think he
will say something?' 'Probably. But not to the rest of the kids.'
'What shall I do?'

'Nothing. I'll deal with it. Leave it to me. You better get
back now.' 'Okay.'

'I love you, you know.' 'So do I, pretzel.'

'You go left, I'll go right.' At which point Des and Julie
appear on either side of me and both immediately stop in
their tracks, startled.

* * *

I'm in the table tennis room, playing ping-pong with Des. My
mate. My close mate. My close mate who has been sleeping
with Julie since God knows when.

'Over to you, back to me,' I say. 'And if anyone walks in,
then whoever has got the ball smashes it real hard to warn the
other to shut up. Okay?'

'Okay,' says Des. 'Good. Your serve.'

'Well, she started it. Not me. Actually, that's wrong. We
both started it... Well...'

'When?'

'Don't know, we just got closer and closer. It was natural...'
'When did it happen?'

'Three months ago.' 'Three months ago?'

'Yeah. I was going to tell you but...you mustn't tell a
soul.' 'What about Barry. Does he know?'

'Julie thinks so. He won't go near her at the moment. You
know they haven't had sex for three years?'

'Really.'

'She hates him,' Des continues. 'She said he was all right when they met. Then she got pregnant with Belinda so they had to marry. But he drinks all the time and he never takes her out. You know when we see him going off in the car? You know when he says he's got to pick up something? Do you know where he's going? He goes to that pub at the top of the hill. Then he drives home pissed.'

'So – what – you and Julie snog and…' 'Yes,' Des pauses. 'And more.'

I can't believe it. Des is no longer a virgin. I am; he isn't. What's more, he has done it with Julie, the mother of the house, the one who said she would stand by me until I went to university, the one who is in her thirties. I can't believe it, I really can't.

'Where?'

'You know that conservatory they've built onto the dining room? In there one night. That was the first time.'

'You're joking. And no one caught you?'

He stops and looks at me. 'Where else?' I ask. 'In the grounds a couple of times.'

I can't believe it. In the grounds. That makes Julie one of us, one of the kids.

'We did go to the boiler room one night but you and Martin were in there having a fag, so we couldn't.'

I start laughing. The whole thing sounds unbelievable.

'She's going to divorce Barry. We may go and live together.' My smile stops. I don't like Des now. I don't like him because he has kept secrets from me. He is not the Des I thought I knew. There is another Des in existence and I have never met him. This Des I haven't spent so many pleasurable hours with, listening to records or sitting on beds, talking books, talking as always about music which is shaping our characters only we don't know it yet. There is a secretive Des who has not shown himself to me, a worldly Des and the only person in the world who knows this Des is Julie. And she has taken him away from me. Once more, that bitter terrain which is the distance between people's words and their real actions is revealed to me.

But I am not surprised. All that time ago when Barry and Julie promised they would stand by me, there was a part of me that never truly believed them. Too many people in the past had laid such promises at my feet and then trampled on them. It was the way of the world. And now Barry and Julie were splitting up. More broken promises. I only hated Des and Julie that night for making me see that again.

Julie was no longer the distant mother. She was human, terribly human. Somewhere along the line her life had become such that she had felt forced to take a very dangerous path to make it better. That's how much she hated Barry and how much she hated not being in love, not being held, not being cherished. And she knew, although she denied it to herself time and time again, that her actions could only lead to bringing about a huge change to all of our lives. I still had no idea that worse, much worse, was yet to come.

'I think I love her,' Des said.

I smashed the ball hard and it flew over the green table. Des looked at me.

'My game. I win,' he said.

* * *

He did it, he really did. Enzo Esposito became the first boy in our year to lose that which tormented and teased and cursed and obsessed every one of us. He went with a girl. Her name was Cathy. She was from our year and the story was instantly verified by her mates, some of whom made out they were shocked but all of whom were secretly thrilled.

Cathy had been lent the keys to her mate's house. The family was away the whole weekend. Amazing. Enzo got to do it over and over again in absolute comfort and peace. Plus, Cathy was a peach of a girl. She had appeared in all our fevered dreams, of that I am certain. Enzo's success stopped all the boys in their tracks. It silenced them and it shamed them. Not me, though.

For the past year, I had watched them coming into school every Monday morning, casually boasting about their weekend conquests. These boys did it everywhere. They did it with girls in discotheques and youth clubs. They stood against walls and they slid into alleyways. They lay down in church graveyards and they scored on the local football pitch. They did it behind shops and they did it in the local park. They did it in cars and they did it in black, bare fields with only the moon as their witness. These acts were never discussed in full. Names and details were simply and casually given and that was all.

'Yeah, picked a girl up Friday. Down at the disco.' 'What school she go to?'

'Winston Churchill.' A girl from a different school always made the story far more exotic. Not only had you scored but you had entered someone else's territory and conquered. Impressive.

'Yeah, got a shag off her.' 'Where?'

'That pub, the Two Feathers. Behind there.' 'You're joking.' 'I'm not.'

'Yeah? I got a shag as well.' 'Really?'

'Minge and everything.'

And then Enzo came along and silenced every one of them. For how could you lie in his presence? He had been to wonderland, had made the journey we had all agonisingly failed to master. No way could you bullshit with him in the room. You simply had to shut up and hope and pray that your turn came soon.

Ironically, considering I was the impoverished one who had neither money nor wardrobe, nor the opportunity to stay out late, it was me who was actually the closest to losing that which tortured us all. In fact, I could have easily beaten Enzo to the punch.

If only I could have figured out how to make Emily say that magic word, yes.

* * *

At the end of September, my social worker and I went again to my mother's hospital. She had been moved to a smaller building in the grounds which meant we didn't have to walk the corridor of horrors any more. Instead, we met in the reception area and were taken to her by a silent nurse. Miss Benkins was too busy to see us.

As usual, my mother was well dressed and nicely made up. She always was when I came to visit. I never saw her careless or unruly in her wardrobe. She had once been a participant in Sorrento's eternal procession. She knew the value of clothes. This day, she was wearing a blue cardigan with a pink stripy T-shirt and a long, grey skirt. She smiled a lot through ruby-painted lips. She always tried to be cheerful around me.

'Hello, Paolo, hello.'

We walked out to the car, 'Oh lovely car, lovely car,' she said. She sat in the front seat and looked so happy to be back in the world again. We drove into the small town nearby to find a restaurant. Free from the grinding drudgery that marked her hours in the hospital, she revelled for a while in her bright surroundings. Being treated like an adult opened her up a little. At the table, she confessed to us that she hated everyone at the hospital. That's why she went to bed at seven at night. She would rather dream her life away than accept the situation. She said she used to go to mass every week in the little church nearby but on Christmas Eve last year, the day of her birthday, the priest had not served communion correctly. That was it, she said, her face creasing up with reproach at the memory of the holy man's blunder. She would never go back to his church. Never. Until they brought in someone else, she would make her own dialogue with God. I suspected she might still have a lot to say to Him.

I recall that lunch well, for it was the first time I got a glimpse of my mother's life and, as a consequence, found myself drawing closer to her. This is how my social worker remembers it:

'Mrs Hewitt's existence in the hospital is not a happy one and she did indicate that in the cycle of twelve months she would only leave the hospital on two day trips, one in the summer – she has recently been to Brighton – and one at Christmas time. One wonders how much of this grieves Paolo.'

I'll be honest here. Despite our growing closer, I still felt a million miles away from my mother. I had tried hard to find my feelings towards her, I really had. On every visit to her, I kept thinking to myself, this is your mother, this is your mother. But nothing connected, nothing came through. My mother was a strange little lady I went to see once in a while. That was all. But after that lunch, I saw us now moving closer together. The social worker continues:

'Over lunch Mrs Hewitt talked about her husband and the trips they had made whilst aboard the ship. Paolo seemed interested in this and, on leaving Mrs Hewitt, he stated that he would not like to live the rest of his life without knowing more about his father.'

As my mama relived the years that had been gracious enough to let her fall in love, visions of my father sprang again to my mind. I saw him tall with a strong, confident demeanour. He wore a loud, red-checked shirt and dark-blue Levis jeans. His hair was like mine, dark and wavy, and his face was middle-aged, craggy, handsome. As I looked upon him, with his one foot standing on a rock, his right arm resting on his right leg and his face directly smiling at me, a luxuriant forest of green and blue behind him, his clothes suddenly changed. They melted away and so did time. I saw him now in his army uniform walking with my mother arm-in-arm through Sorrento, that little town of magic. He takes her in his arms and they dance upon cobbled streets, holding each other firm.

The picture dissolves. They are now on the ship to South Africa, standing at the front facing out, both of them smoking their cigarettes, dissolving into each other with every smile. He wears a dark suit and his hair is slicked back to reveal his strong features. My mother wears a simple printed dress upon which her dark hair lightly dances in the wind. In front of them the huge yellow sun bows in honour to their beauty and illuminates their every expectation. Love sparkles on the waves.

Switch. I see them landing in England, disembarking, carrying luggage in their arms. Fog swirls around them, eating them up until they vanish from view, lost to the fates of their own lives. The report concludes:

'I said to Paolo that we would discuss his father on my next meeting, whilst in the interim I would try and get some helpful details about him. Paolo commented that he had enjoyed the trip and what a success it had been.'

Meanwhile, unknown to me at the time, my social worker had made contact with my two sisters. And now she was on the trail of my father who had escaped to Canada. Slowly, the broken circle was starting to come together.

* * *

Rosie became a full-time staff member and moved into the bedroom on the top floor. Her room was in the middle of two bedrooms, us boys on one side and Val and Esther on the other. Across the tiny landing was Kim and Emily's bedroom. We had stopped visiting them. Cruelly, Val had gone to Barry and told him of our midnight trips. She had split on us, told him everything. As she lay in bed, she had heard our padding feet, the discreet closing of doors, the moans of lust and frustration.

I was furious. To split on someone is to declare an act of war. Typical of her middle-class upbringing, I thought. What a prude. But I couldn't hate her. Val was fifteen years old but she was going on twenty-five. She had to be for Roger, her younger brother, who walked around the Home still dazed by his sudden change in circumstances. How cruel his fate. One day he was an ordinary boy from an ordinary middle-class background in an ordinary middle-class school and then, without even a warning shot to alert him, he fell to the lowest rung of the ladder. Their father was a high flyer in a uniform who was stationed abroad. Their mum had tended to them in a leafy and desirable suburb. Their world was secure and prosperous. It was solid, it was how it was meant to be. Suddenly, they were motherless. She passed away. The father couldn't come home. If he did he would lose his job. Now his children were laying down their heads in an orphanage. How cruel the world must have seemed to them both at that time, how devastating in its arbitrary choice as to who should suffer and who not. Is luck the only protection we have against life?

Val had taken it upon herself to protect her younger brother, to comfort him, to try and make sense of the life they now lived for him. Which was fine and noble and as it should be. But who was there to comfort her? No one. And lack of love, like lack of food, does strange things to people. One day, Val went to Barry and told him all about our visits to Kim and Emily. Barry listened and he listened and then he said, 'Right,' and he stormed out of the room and he dragged Martin and me to the back sitting room to roar at us. Yet his rage at our behaviour seemed tame. I was a veteran of his anger, knew that dark turbulent temper so well. But this time, the taste was different. Oh he did the normal routine of ranting, pressing his face close to ours, arm-waving, but you could sense his heart wasn't really in the performance. At the time, I thought it was because he knew he was being a true hypocrite. All those hours spent lusting after big-bosomed actresses on TV, all those lusty laughs in the car as he sped past a puzzled young girl, all that egging us on – what did he expect? Now, though, I see his mind was obviously elsewhere. It was not on us or the Home. It was on a wife shrinking from his view day by day by day.

Straight after the bollocking, I sought out Val. She was standing in the kitchen by the oven, waiting for her soup to boil. She was in her school uniform, tall and lanky, and as I walked purposefully towards her my eyes strayed towards her long legs.

'I want to talk to you.' I put my face up close to hers. 'Why did you split on me and Martin to Barry?' I demanded.

She looked at me coolly and then gave me an answer I shall never forget.

'Because you never came to visit me,' she simply said.

* * *

Rosie moved in next to Val and brought along with her the songwriters Bob Dylan, Tim Hardin, David Ackles and Neil Young. She also brought in the writers Jack Kerouac, Ken Kesey, John Fowles, Michael Herr, Allen Ginsberg, Truman Capote, Norman Mailer and Tom Wolfe. They were nice guys. They all said hello to me as they moved their stuff in.

Her room was small and she lit it low. There was a bed in one corner and a dark, ugly wardrobe in the other. Next to the bed, on the cheap, blue carpet, was her record player. It wasn't a hi-fi. It was a red-and-white coloured box with the speaker in the lid. Records sounded great on it. On the table next to her was her picture taken at the Windsor Free Festival. She was standing in jeans and a bikini top and she was smiling. Behind her, lying on the ground and clearly tripping on acid, were two teenagers laughing at the sky.

Rosie played me Bob Dylan and she read me poems. She showed me that failure could be success and that success was no failure at all. She gave me books to read and thoughts to ponder. For me, she looked at life a little askew. Once more, the world I had been urged all my life to inhabit, the one of work and exams and success, had been casually challenged. Everything that my mind had been taught was right and proper by Mrs K. and the teachers at school was not destroyed by Rosie but replaced by something infinitely more exciting. Be happy in yourself, she said, and all things will grow from there. If earning thousands makes you happy, then you do it. If digging roads makes you happy, then try for it. But never put one above the other.

I went to Rosie's room on her nights off. She was quite isolated. She came from Stroud in Gloucestershire and had no friends in town to hang out with. I felt uneasy lying or sitting on her bed so I sat by the box that was her record player and we swapped music. I gave her Rod Stewart; she gave me Van Morrison. I reminded her of how good The Beatles were; she tried to put me onto Joni Mitchell.

'You know, Rod Stewart tried to pick her up once,' I told her as she played me her album, Court and Spark.

'Did he?'

'Oh yeah. Apparently they met in some nightclub and were getting on fine but then some drummer guy showed up. Rod said he had the hairier chest so she went off with him.' I knew this because it had been in the NME that week. Straight from Rod's mouth.

'I hate hairy chests,' Rosie said. My ears pricked up.

I started spending more and more time in that room. It had become a new and welcome place to hide in. For downstairs, things were falling badly apart.

* * *

It's teatime at the Home. Sarah leaves her place and goes to the table by the hatch and picks up a bowl of rice pudding. Jam has been placed in the centre of the rice but it has sunk to the bottom and she doesn't see it. She returns to her table. She sits, dips her spoon into the rice, looks down and stops. 'I don't want jam in my rice pudding,' she says, staring into her bowl.

Julie, whose half-finished plate of food lies pushed away from her, replies, 'You'll have to eat it.'

'I don't want jam. Don't like it.'

'But all the puddings have jam in it.' 'But I want one without the jam.'

A voice suddenly barks out from across the room, determined to cut off this verbal tussle before it escalates any further. 'Right! If that's the way you want it.'

Julie and Sarah both look over at my table. It is Barry. He now stands, goes over to Sarah's table, leans between two children to get to her, picks up her bowl and then softly but deliberately places it upside down on her head. White, gooey rice smeared with red drips down both sides of her face.

Sarah looks at Barry with a vacant expression that lasts for five seconds. The room is deathly quiet, uncomprehending. Then it comes, low at first but gathering pace, finally shaping itself into an almighty huge scream.

Barry stands glaring at her, absolutely unmoved by the noise. 'Shut up,' he snarls. He then looks at Julie and his face is such that everyone who sees it at that precise moment knows its meaning straight away. It says, I wish to God that had been you. And he walks out.

We hear the front door slam and his purple Morris Minor start up. We hear the car reverse back, turn and then roar off. And above it all, we hear Sarah's cry. It is high, piercing, terrible to listen to. But no one stops her. For it is the Home's lament for Barry and Julie's broken marriage, the broken promises and the broken future which now faces us all.

* * *

In school, Mr Doyle stands at the front of the classroom. He is explaining to us the importance of the exams we have coming up next summer. 'If you get five O levels,' he says in his Scottish drawl, 'you can expect to earn about five thousand pounds a year once you start working. Roughly five thousand.' He starts pacing the floor in front of us. He is wearing his normal grey suit and white shirt and blue striped tie. 'If you get five O levels and two A levels,' he says, 'you can expect to earn about eight to ten thousand pounds a year. That would be right.' He turns to face us straight on. 'But if you get a degree, well, the sky's the limit.' He tells us this last fact in a voice which simultaneously manages to suggest both awe at the glittering prize ahead, and his own belief that such knowledge is probably only of use to maybe three or four of the pupils sitting in front of him.

'The sky's the limit.'

Not once, in my five years at school, do I ever hear him equate learning with pleasure.

'Sir,' Pete Garland says from the back of the class, 'what about people who don't get any O levels?' A few of the boys chuckle.

'What about them?' he snaps. 'Now open your books.'

* * *

I walk down the drive in winter on a cold and dark morning and at the end of it I come upon Stephen, standing on the edge of the pavement, nine years old, in his school uniform, watching the cars go by.

'Hello,' I say. 'All right.'

'What you doing?' 'Waiting for my mum.' 'She taking you out today?'

'Nah. Sometimes she drives by here.' Stephen looks away. I follow his gaze. I see a bus appear on the brow of the hill. It slowly plunges down towards us. Stephen shuffles his feet expectantly. As the bus draws near, a woman conductor can be seen inside the vehicle, one hand clutching the vertical rail. She is looking out onto our side of the road. Soon, she will be directly in front of us.

'That's my mum,' Stephen says and he begins waving. But as the bus approaches, the woman does something totally unexpected; she swivels around to face the other side of the road. She sees Stephen, her son, standing on the pavement and she turns her back on him. She does so because she knows that she is weak and she knows that she is cruel. She knows that when her boyfriend said he didn't want Stephen in the flat with him, that he wanted her all to himself, she should have kicked her lover out instead of agreeing to his demands and putting her son into care.

The bus flashes by. Stephen sees nothing but his mother's back. His eyes stay on her until she disappears around the corner. Then he hitches up his satchel, says 'See ya,' turns to the right and begins walking up that hill again.

He'll be back here again tomorrow morning, bright and early.

That lunchtime I am to be found avidly reading the *NME* in the fifth-year cloakroom. It is Thursday, the day copies finally come in from London; the day I always leave the Home early so as to be the first to buy and read it cover to cover. I am fanatical about that paper. The night before I lie in bed wondering what musician will be on the cover and I take bets with myself about it. Then I try to picture what the writers have been doing that week, who they have been talking to, what albums they have been listening to, how they are dressed, what cigarettes they are smoking, what their houses and their girlfriends look like. I have already told the careers officer that this is what I want to do with my life. I want to be a music journalist. I said it at our one and only meeting and he looked at me with a completely uncomprehending gaze.

'A music what?'

'A music journalist.'

'Oh. Doesn't sound very secure. The Civil Service? Have you thought of that?'

The *NME* in those days was like playing a great record. Once is never enough. I am on my second reading of the day and am about to turn a page when the cloakroom doors fly open and Laz and Vic and Enzo barge through, giggling like crazy.

'Give it here, give it here,' Enzo says to Vic. 'Let me have a look.' Vic pulls away from him. 'No, find the sandwiches first.'

'Come on,' Laz says, 'they're bound to be somewhere. Paulo, keep a lookout, make sure Garland is not coming.'

I go to the door whilst the boys start hunting in lockers and feeling along the top of the coat racks. They dip into blazer pockets and they open up sports bags and briefcases in their frantic search. I am still looking out for Pete when I hear Enzo shout, 'Got 'em.' I turn and see him pulling that familiar clear sandwich-box from under some football kit in a Puma bag. 'The cheeky wanker tried to hide them in Tommy O'Sullivan's bag,' Enzo says. His voice has tints of true admiration in it.

Vic now reaches into his pocket and pulls out a square plastic shape. He puts it to his teeth and he rips open the packet. Then he pulls out a shrivelled pink condom. Everyone starts laughing as Vic stretches it wider and wider. 'Okay, give me the sandwiches,' he says. 'What's he got in them?'

'Ham.'

'Perfect, absolutely perfect.'

Pete puts a sandwich to his mouth and two hundred eyes swivel discreetly in his direction. Most of us in the dinner hall are in the know.

It is why we are trying to act normal as we queue up for our slices of lean meat, dollops of cabbage and potato and, best of all, our bowls of chocolate pudding and custard, delivered unto us by the harmless ladies in the plastic hats and the white coats. One of them is Mrs Davis, who is studiously ignoring me. She is the one who innocently handed the trolley over to Enzo and me last year and received a ticking off from Deish for doing so. She has not yet forgiven me. I want to tell her that I sympathise and that she should have heard the verbal vitriol that rained down on my ears, not to mention the detentions I received. But, to be honest, I really can't be bothered.

Pete finishes his sandwich, stops eating and starts talking to the other five boys round his table. He is totally at ease. We know this because before lunch he had already expressed his joy and delight at our apparent inability to find his lunch.

'That's because I put them,' he told us, holding the sandwiches in front of us and mimicking the group Slade and their latest single – 'far, far, away.'

'Yeah, that's right, Pete,' we replied, hoping we looked suitably defeated by his cleverness. 'Beat us today.'

Pete now sits at his table, unsuspecting. Two of the boys he is nattering to are the Bloan twins. One of them has just discovered that God, for some unfathomable reason, has only blessed him with one testicle.

For the last week, the boys in the class have been really, really sympathetic.

Every time he comes near them on the playground, they sing, 'Bloany has only got one ball. The other is in the Albert Hall. His mother, his dirty mother, she nicked it when he was small.'

Pete pulls out a second sandwich. A frisson of discreet nudges and nods surround him but he remains oblivious to the silent commotion. He raises the sandwich to his mouth. We all take a silent breath. He bites into the sandwich. Something is not right. He pulls at it again. His teeth are entangled on something, something pink. Slowly, the pink starts stretching from his mouth. It goes further and further and further… Pete stops and he noisily spits out the offending article. He shouts 'What the hell was that?' The other boys at his table stare at him in wonderment. The teacher on dinner duty, who is sitting by the dinner-hall door reading a newspaper, quickly looks up. He puts down the paper and starts ambling over to Pete's table to see what the commotion is all about.

I can't bear it. I turn away. Me, Vic, Laz and Enzo are absolutely creased up. So is everyone else around me. This is better than what we had planned because now Pete Garland has to explain to Mr Doyle, the deputy head of a Catholic school, what a half-chewed condom is doing on his dinner table.

* * *

I had decided to become a music journalist. I told no one because I knew they would think it a ridiculous ambition. But

I didn't. I loved music and I loved books. Both were equally magical because both allowed me – encouraged me, even – to forget the world. When I wasn't being lifted by music I was stuck in a book. At other times, I daydreamed about reading every book that was ever written. Music journalism might have been a very long shot to aim for, but as soon as the idea had stuck inside my head it gave me something that I had lacked up until then: a direction. I began to act upon the dream.

First, I tried to join the girls' typing class. Someone had come up with the bright idea that one afternoon a week girls could do boys' subjects and we in turn could take lessons such as home economics. 'Can we play netball as well, miss?' a newly arrived pupil, Geoff Loughton, asked when the scheme was unveiled to us one afternoon.

'No, that won't be necessary,' Mrs Gardiner said tartly.

I went for typing. On the given afternoon, I made my way to the top floor of the school and walked into a class where thirty girls and a teacher turned to look at me.

'Yes, Hewitt?' said Mrs Briggs.

I was mortified to be challenged so publicly. 'I want to learn typing, miss.'

'Oh. You do. Okay. Well…' Mrs Briggs looked around the class, obviously surprised that a boy would desire such a thing. It didn't chime with her. You learnt the typewriter to become a secretary and it was girls who became secretaries. Not boys. Simple. Now I had complicated things.

'Uh… I am afraid there's not enough typewriters to go round.' 'Oh,' I replied, eager now to get away, eager as ever to acquiesce to anyone in charge. 'Okay. I'll go.' Which I did. I turned, flushed with red, and left the class. Later I heard from one of the girls present that Mrs Briggs thought I was there to ogle the girls. I wasn't. I was there because I wanted to be a writer. Mrs Briggs simply didn't have the love to see that.

My next move was to set up a business amongst my friends. For fifty pence, I offered to write their essays or read their books. My first job was for Vic, 200 words on 'Why I Should be More Respectful to Adults.' My next job was for Laz. He handed me a book he was about to be tested on the following morning. He asked me to read it for him. I did. In a night. He passed.

Business was booming but I wasn't. My own school workload, coupled with that of half of my classmates', proved too much. Reluctantly, I shut up shop. In retaliation to this failure, I started walking round school with a copy of Plato's *The Republic* under my arm. Others showed off their records. Too easy for me. I opted for an ancient Greek philosopher.

'Enjoying that, are you?' my English teacher asked one day. 'Yes, miss. Fascinating.'

'Good, you can tell me all about it after class.' Her name was Miss Woodhead. She was a spinster who lived with her mother in a bungalow up near my old primary school. Every night, she went home and tended to her. Then she read Shakespeare until bedtime. That was her life, she proudly told us, apart from the two weeks they took every year to travel to New York and visit her brother, a lawyer. 'We visited when Watergate was happening,' she breathlessly told us once in class. 'My brother would come home after working twelve hours and then sit in front of the TV not talking to any of us, just absolutely fascinated by it all.' She sighed in a kind of blissful admiration for her brother's rudeness. Miss Woodhead was an academic of the highest order but a teacher of the worst kind. She could not hide either the smugness that marks many people of high intelligence or her impatience at those who struggled behind her. She was middle-aged with stern, tight-brown eyes, glasses and pinned-back grey hair. Her favourites were the brainy girls, the chaste-looking ones at the front of the class who did their homework in neat writing. She had very little time for boys. They unnerved her. They were usually the source of all trouble.

As the class filed out that day, I sat at my desk, pensive, wary. I hadn't read a word of Plato. I hadn't checked one sentence from the book that I brandished every day at school like a badge. If she asked me one question about the book I would be stuck for words.

'Sit by my desk,' she said.

I walked up and drew a chair near to her. I noticed her stubby fingers and felt her nervousness. She and I were sitting in an empty classroom, and close proximity to another human being always makes the aloof terribly uneasy.

'I have to tell you that your performance in the mock exams was not very good,' she revealed. 'Not very good at all. You are what we call a "late developer" but even so I did have some expectation of success from you in your English subjects.' She put her closed hands in front of her face. Protection. 'Is there any reason for this lapse? How are things at home?' she asked me.

Straight away, I said, 'Fine. Everything is fine. Good.' It was my defence mechanism. Been with me all my life. Agree with everything and cover up the rest. That way conflict is unlikely to arise. You don't want to meet the ghost of Mrs K. now.

'Are you sure?'

Her concern for me felt awfully thin. She knew it as well. I was not one of her favoured elite and compassionate enquiry into another's fate was never really her forte. I knew that if, at that moment, I had told her about Barry and Julie and Des or how confused about my past and worried about my future I was, she would have run a mile. She wasn't equipped to deal with human emotions. Miss Woodhead knew life through Shakespeare. She never lived it.

'Well, why is your work slipping? You were on track three months ago.'

'I don't know, miss. I will try harder. I will.'

'Well, you had better if you want to pass your O levels. Have you thought about what you want to do in the future?'

Normally, I would have replied, 'I'd like to be a teacher.' But for some reason, maybe a desire to liven things up, I decided to gamble on her decision to look into me.

'Yes, I want to be a music journalist.'

Miss Woodhead didn't reply. I realised she didn't know what a music journalist was.

'I want to write for a music paper and...' 'Write? You?'

And then she laughed. It was a short laugh, a bitter laugh but it was a laugh I have never, ever forgotten. It shot out from her tight mouth and in a second it had not only mocked my dream, it had nearly destroyed it.

Twenty-five years later I heard that laugh again when I agreed to attend my school's twenty-fifth anniversary reunion.

'Will a Miss Woodhead be there?' I asked. I wanted to take the eight books I had written by then and place each one directly in front of her eyes. That's how much I hated her for that laugh.

'No, sadly Miss Woodhead passed away last year.'

Time makes you old too soon, smart too late and, as part of the deal, it also robs you of the chance for revenge.

'Teaching would be a good option for you,' she offered that day in the classroom, but I wasn't listening. I couldn't. My soul was too busy absorbing the knife she had thrust into me so callously.

That day I decided to keep my dream silent from everyone. That night, I decided to go it alone, for I had learnt my true lesson. The less you give people, the less they have to hurt you with. From now on, I would tell the teachers that my ambition was to be a teacher. That would satisfy everyone concerned. They would like that. A teacher. That would be good. It meant that this looked after kid they taught was a success of theirs; that he hadn't got ideas too far above his station.

* * *

Barry and Julie decided not to make a public announcement about their marriage breaking up. Instead, they decided to let the news filter down to us. They were too taken up with their own lives to do anything else. Barry was taking a new job in Epsom. Julie, her daughter Belinda, and Des (who was old enough to leave care now) were going to move in together in a flat in town. Des informed me of their decision one night in the boiler room. We both smoked our cigarettes casually now, not even bothering to keep a watch out for a staff member who might scold us for our actions. Barry and Julie's imminent departure had let loose feelings of recklessness within us all.

'We found a place near the cop shop,' Des told me, 'it's a lovely flat. You can visit us.'

'That's handy,' I said. 'Maxwells is opposite. You can get all your guitar strings in there.' A brief laugh but not enough to bridge the gap between us. If the truth be told, Des was a million miles away from me now. He was doing adult things. He was moving into a flat, taking on a lover and a daughter. He was moving into a different world, one that I couldn't even dream about inhabiting. It was so far away, so distant. 'You should come and visit,' he repeated.

I said I would but I never did. I left them to it. Instead, I spent those last days of their command wondering if Barry and Julie would privately talk to me about what was happening. If they did, I mused, what excuse would they have for letting me down, for not staying with me until I left the Home, as they had promised so many times? The answer never came. They ignored me just as they ignored everyone else. One day I woke up and they were gone, just like all the others, like Tommy and Colin and Frank and Terry and all the others who had passed like ghosts before my eyes. Sometimes, at night, I wondered if these people had ever existed.

They sent in new leaders for us dislocated discontents. First came Mary and her two cats. She was only a temporary measure, a useless stop-gap. The Home was unsteady now, unsure of direction and purpose. All of us felt betrayed, angry, listless. Such feelings were creeping into every crevice of the place. Soon, they would tear this house of good and bad down to the ground.

Mary, as expected, lasted two months. (In my files it notes that 'Paolo had been asked to take the prospective new house mother around the Home and had been very aware that he was full of hostility and resentment towards her and had treated her in a very discourteous manner.') Then came a Mr Ella. He used to be in the army. According to the files he wasn't too happy with me either. 'Mr Ella seemed to be of the opinion that Paolo was creating havoc,' it says. I know why he thought this. He thought this because one night I went to a party and I drank beer and I drank Martini and I threw up and then I walked to a phone and I rang him and I told him I needed to stay at my friend's house that night. He told me I couldn't. I put the phone down on him. Then I called him back. 'I'm fucking staying,' I told him. I came home sober the next day and we avoided each other. I shrugged my shoulders and went to the boiler room to smoke a cigarette and fight the first hangover of my life. 'House father,' my file notes, 'sounded very agitated, not to say a little out of control…he was using phrases such as, "It's a battleground out here… "'

It wasn't. It was me and Martin and everyone else doing what we wanted and not giving one monkey if anyone objected or not.

One night, Sarah climbed through the window of the boys' bedroom on the top floor and out onto a ledge on the roof. Pete Mac was called to save her. He coaxed her back in, talking gently, softly and with a compassion she could not fail to hear. The next day the builders arrived to put locks on the windows. Mr Ella looked even more worried as he supervised them. The Home was not my home any more. Like all else in this world, it had proved itself transient. My social worker makes a visit.

'A rather explosive, angry interview…prior to his angry outburst, he talked in a superficial way about his inability to make meaningful relationships with people. He imagines he has been disappointed by so many people that the result has been to make him hollow and empty inside…he spoke with vehemence about social workers "probing" and stated that all he wanted was to be left alone…he continued in this vein by saying that everyone had used him and so he wanted to use someone…'

And that's what I did do. I began to use everyone who came into my path. I took them for everything I could. I pushed all their buttons. If I was told off at school I would blame the action on being an orphan. If someone showed me kindness, I would spit in their face. I chased every girl and tried to break every heart. People, beware the stricken and the unhappy, for theirs is the sweetest revenge of all.

Within a month, Mr Ella surrendered and was on his way. The authorities finally saw sense. Pete Mac was put in charge of the Home and life now settled down. Martin and I rubbed our hands together when we heard the news. Pete was extremely fond of us both. He loved our cheekiness, the way that when he told us off for not cleaning up our bedroom or doing some menial job, we would stand there and say, 'Sorry, Pete,' and then together put our tongues firmly in our cheeks and glance at each other. Pete knew what we were doing.

'You little buggers, you stop mucking around and listen to me,' he'd shout but the laughter in his eyes betrayed him. He took us to meet his mother and hang out in his home. He introduced us to his circle of friends and he made clear his conditions – You two are older. I've got enough on my hands with the little ones. Play it cool for me, okay? As a sign of his trust, he passed us the keys to the front door. We were sixteen and we were free to come and go as we pleased. Now we could start behaving properly.

* * *

Bob Dylan was singing 'You're A Big Girl Now' when I first kissed Rosie. It was five in the morning. We had stayed up talking about the Home and Barry and Julie and Des and so on and so on until the sun was knocking on the window, anxious to break up our words and start another day. We were sat on her bed and suddenly we were kissing. Immediately, I pushed my hand inside her blouse to feel those breasts of hers. I rubbed her bra. Nervous. We were both so nervous. She pulled back and, looking me in the eyes, she unbuttoned her shirt. The cheesecloth fell away like curtains. Then she put her arms behind her back and undid her bra strap. Her breasts fell loose and for the first time ever they offered themselves to me. I fell onto them, suckling her for comfort as much as for pleasure. I pushed her back on the bed. I eagerly clasped onto her breasts with my mouth. My other hand went for her mound. I stupidly tried to push in between her skin and the tightness of her jeans. As I struggled, and as I kissed her, I heard a zip being lowered and a button popping. My eyes remained closed but my fingers were free now. I pushed downwards and I found her centre. I could not believe what was happening to me.

I pulled out my hand from her trousers. I quickly fumbled with my trousers and pants. I was sure she was going to stop me as all the others had. I pulled them down and threw them aside. Then I lay on top of her. For one brief second, I realised that I was about to rid myself of my virginity. Then I pushed myself into her sea of velvet and felt for the very first time sparks of pure absolute pleasure shoot into every part of my body. In an incredulous state of mind, I moved and I moved. Five seconds later I was spent. Two minutes later I was in my bed. Dazed.

* * *

Pete Mac had given me my freedom and I took full advantage of it. I stayed out late, went out often. And I visited Rosie whenever I could. I never told Martin about my clandestine canoodlings. I never told a soul. I loved the idea of operating in absolute secrecy, of being above suspicion. I now felt the thrill Des and Julie must have experienced and I forgave them. Plus, as Rosie strongly insisted, information in the hands of

others was too dangerous to risk. This was her career that was
at stake. I must tell no one, not even my closest link, Martin. It
wasn't too much of a hard task to keep quiet. At this particular
juncture in our lives, I was seeing less of him than usual. It
wasn't through change or arguing. It was because Martin had
landed a part-time job directly over the road, working in the
antique shop. The experience was changing him.

He would now come home and excitedly tell me how he
and his boss Andy had gone round some old widow's house,
taken her valuable furniture and paid her a tenner for the
goods.

'Well,' Andy the boss would say, 'if that's what they think
it's worth who am I to tell them differently?'

I couldn't agree. The whole thing felt wrong to me. My
way of thinking had been immeasurably strengthened by my
talks with Rosie. I had been drawn to her because of her
body but now I was exposed to her mind. I visited her room
at least three times a week. I loved my time there. I loved the
education she was giving me and I loved the danger of our
going to bed together. I understood now as I never could
before why Des was so intoxicated by his relationship with
Julie. The whiff of danger is seduction itself.

Once, on one of Rosie's afternoons off, when we were
halfway through a session, Pete Mac came to her door. He
knocked gently. 'Rosie,' he said, 'Rosie.'

I slid out of bed and went, as prearranged, to the wardrobe,
where I hid behind its open door. I saw Rosie pull on her
striped top, shouting, 'Yeah, be with you in a minute' as she
struggled with her jeans.

She got up and opened the door and straight away Pete
said, 'Are you on your own? I thought I heard someone else
in here.'

'No,' Rosie said, 'just me. Little old me.'

'I wouldn't call you little, dear,' Pete replied cheekily, before asking, 'Um, do you know where the duty roster is?'

'Eh, yes, it's in the kitchen. I'll come down and get it for you. I was going to make a cup of tea anyway. Would you like one?'

'Thanks. By the way, you haven't seen Paulo anywhere, have you?'

I heard the door shut and I heard fate clump down the stairs. To this day I don't know if Pete knew I was there. He never said a word to me either way. All I know was that I was dressed and out of Rosie's room in one minute and forty-two seconds precisely.

All in all, my thing with Rosie was great. Yet I couldn't just enjoy it like Martin would have done. I had to worry myself about it. I had to question it, analyse it, rob it of its excitement and purpose. In other words, I had to destroy it because it was good and I only understood bad. I began thinking our sex wasn't going anywhere. I loved handling and kissing her large, round breasts. I loved pushing into her and feeling the spark of life ignite my body. I loved the warmth of our skin together but I couldn't ignore how awkward we were when we coupled. It put me off and I began thinking that I should finish it.

Such were the thoughts that were messing with my mind one afternoon when I was waiting for my social worker to visit. Strangely, she had called a week earlier and arranged to see me. I remember thinking at the time that I wasn't due to see her for another week but I didn't say anything. She was probably coming to pick up the pieces after my last outburst. I didn't care. If she wanted to hear me say sorry, then I would. But I wasn't going to open up to her. I wasn't going to open up to anyone. Unless there was something in it for me.

That day, the Home was empty save for me and Agassi, a new member of staff. Martin and myself had been tormenting her lately. Agassi had recently let slip that she was the niece of the director of Social Services. This information explained everything. Agassi was absolutely hopeless at her job. She had no idea about kids or how to deal with them. And looked after kids are like all other kids; we smell blood a mile away. Agassi tried to be tough with us and we burst out laughing. She tried to be funny and we looked at her blankly. Mostly, though, we ignored her. The little ones soon cottoned on as well. They gave her the runaround like only four-year-olds can. They drove her mad. Sarah, in fact, said no to her all the time. Whatever Agassi's question, her answer would be exactly the same.

'Go to bed.' 'No.'

'Go for a bath.' 'No.'

'Want some chocolate?' 'No.'

'How old are you?' 'No.'

If Agassi had one saving grace it was that she smoked incessantly, which meant that behind her back Martin and I were able to dip into the various packets of Embassy Regals she left in the sitting room or in her handbag.

That day, Agassi was in her room developing her nicotine moustache, and Pete, plus his new lieutenants, Linda and Dom, had taken most of the kids swimming. Martin was over the road getting fed bullshit about the importance of money and I was listening to an album called 'Sunny Afternoon' by The Kinks. It was on the cheap MFP label. Ray Davies was singing 'Dead End Street' when I heard a car pulling up on the drive outside. I stood up, went over and looked out through the open window. My social worker was getting out of the taxi, the back door of the car being held open by a small, burly man wearing a dark leather jacket that clashed with his immense shock of white hair. I saw my social worker pass him a leaf of green.

'This is where they live then, is it?' I heard him ask as he pocketed the money. He looked towards the house. 'Poor little sods,' he said with genuine feeling.

Poor little sods. It was a good description.

He moved back to the driver's seat but my social worker stopped him. 'Eh, sorry – excuse me, but my change,' she said.

He stopped and threw his hands up in the air. 'I am so forgetful these days,' he said turning back to her. 'Sorry, love, must be my age, eh?'

He reached deep into his pockets, brought up some silver pearls and handed them over. 'Nearly got away with it,' he said, laughing. My social worker smiled, turned and walked towards the door. I nodded to her. She waved back and I met her by the front door. Here we go round the mulberry bush again.

'Well, hello there,' she said, stepping onto the hall's marbled floor. 'We can go in here,' I said curtly, directing her to the conservatory that had just been built onto the side of the dining room. 'Okay.'

We settled down on chairs facing each other. Despite the sun outside, there was a kind of gloom in the room. It was emanating from her.

'I have some news for you and I am afraid it is not good.'

I had seen the films. I knew the routine. Someone had died. But who? 'It's your father.'

Christ, not him. Please. I hadn't met him yet. You couldn't take him away from me. Not now. Then I realised I was mistaken; that this was something far more serious. The colour of her voice told me that. It was beyond shocked, it was disbelieving.

'I don't know how to put this,' she continued. I could see how nervous she was. 'About six months ago you started talking about wanting to know more about your father. I began looking into your request. I have spent some time going through the relevant files and...'

She paused and then I saw all the air in her body fly out. 'The man you think is your father? He's not. He is Nina and Frankie's father. Not yours. He left your mother before you were born. We don't know who your father is or where he is now. All we know is that he worked at the hospital where your mother has been all these years. I really don't know much more than that.'

The ground beneath my feet gave way and I plummeted downwards. I bounced off walls. No gravity could stop me, no force was on my side. I felt stab wounds in my soul and I looked down and saw my heart turn black. Down and down I plunged, to the very bottom of the world and there I came to lie.

Hey, look at me, Ma. I'm at the bottom of the world.

I heard a voice from above. I looked up and saw words, useless words, pretty words, sad words, compassionate words, big words, small words tumble down towards me, scattering everywhere around me. They came from my social worker and they said that my father either worked at the hospital or he was a patient. No one knew for sure. In fact, in the days leading up to my birth the hospital had no idea that my mother was pregnant. They thought she had put on weight. That was all. No one suspected a thing and she certainly never said a word.

It was only five days before my birth – repeat, five days – that the truth became known. My mother was pregnant. This was on 7 July 1958, and the question on everyone's mind was – who is the father? They asked my mother several times.

She simply laughed at them. First she said it was him. Then she said no, it was the other one. Then she changed her story again. In fact every time they asked who the father was, she gave them a different name. I still haven't figured out why she didn't give over my father's name.

Maybe she was madly in love with him and knew what would happen if she gave him up. Or maybe my mother felt so triumphant at fooling them, of defying them, of lying to them, of scaring them for what they had done to her, that her refusal to name him was her bitter triumph, a payback against those who had imprisoned her. My mother was ill but she was not as ill as those who stood in that corridor of horror fighting thin air and the demons that dance in front of their eyes only. She knew it, we all knew it. My mother should never have been put under lock and key. She should have been given counsel and advice when her husband left her. Someone should have taken care. But no one did and by the time we had entered the frame of her life, it was too late to save her. She had been put on drugs that she could now not do without. They had her. But my mother refused to lie down. Now she had fought back. She had scandalised her oppressors. She knew that if word of the birth got out to a wider world, then boiling outrage would pour down on the hospital. Heads would have to roll. Questions would be asked, inquiries launched. Those in charge scrambled for cover. Files were discreetly replaced. Everything was hushed up. And then I came into the world, the dummy they duped, the one they never told the truth to.

More words tumbled towards me. I reached out and caught them, assembled them in my hands and held them up to the light. At the time, these words told me Miss Benkins worked at the hospital.

'Do you recall on your first visit that she told you not to ask your mother about your father? It wasn't because it might upset her. It was because you might discover the truth.'

I was staring at my social worker but in truth I was staring at nothing except the image in my mind of being eight years old again, alone in my bedroom. There are red weals on my body where I have been caned and outside the rain is smashing into my window and the tree outside is the Devil tapping on the glass trying to get in and I feel for the very first time that all-devouring sense of the world utterly abandoning me.

And now, as I faced my shaken social worker, I felt again that feeling which I thought I had lost forever.

I never thought again of the man in the loud, red-checked shirt and the blue Levis jeans who lived in Canada and smiled at me in front of the huge forest. Never.

And that's the thing about being crushed by life. It's not enough to experience it. It takes your dreams away as well.

For me, my files reveal the best bit of the whole story; the icing on the cake. They state that on the actual night of my birth, my mother's husband, the man I had dreamed of as my father for so many years, called the hospital. He wanted to inquire about my mother's health. Not because he was thinking about her – but because he wanted a divorce. The nurse who answered the phone was as innocent as me: 'Yes, Mr Hewitt, your wife is fine and doing well. She's gone into labour so it won't be too long now. She's doing fine. There's nothing to worry about.' 'Sorry?'

'She's in labour now. Won't be too long and then you'll be a father again.'

Mr Hewitt put the phone down and he laughed out loud. He didn't even have to ask my mother anything. He was ecstatic. He had his grounds for a divorce.

I awoke on a sea of sapphire, adrift from it all. Time was not my friend nor my enemy. It was neither fast nor slow. I spent days sat by the record player and I spent it playing and dreaming of the long and winding road, wondering where on this earth it would next take me. Not that I cared. 'Many times,' Paul sang, 'I've been alone' – and I knew more than anyone else the force behind those words. I let no one come near me and I sought no counsel. I was sullen on the outside, shattered on the inside. I needed no human being. When the world has betrayed you twice how can a mortal mend that which the very gods have made so? I sat alone as I did so many times. I didn't even cry. For tears couldn't even begin to help me.

According to my files:

'He appears to be going through a very anxious and even depressed period but he glosses over these feelings with a patina of confidence and ability that he acknowledges is his method of coping.'

Later on in life, my mother will sit in the front of a car driven by my brother-in-law and, for only the second time in her life, she will turn to me and tell me my father's name.

'Your father's name was Cruise, Mr Cruise. Sorry, Paolo, sorry.' She can remember my father's surname but not his Christian name. Perhaps she never knew it.

'What was he, Mama?' I press her. 'Was he English, Irish, Italian? What?'

Her face drops. 'I don't know. Sorry, Paolo, sorry.'

I know it kills my mother to wound her son like this, not to be able to tell him who his father was, what he was like and where he was from. It is because of the fog that is now her mind.

I know it kills her that I live in a Home and that I have never felt her love. I know she feels pain at the life I have had to live without her. I know she despairs that she was not the one to love me, protect me, to raise me with love and strength.

I know all this for I see it in that place in her dark, jewelled eyes which no pill can extinguish.

She looks at me quizzically and she says sorry again. My heart breaks. I instinctively lean forward and pat her shoulders, rub them a little.

'Niente problema,' I lie to her in Italian, 'niente problema.'

She turns and gazes at the road speeding underneath her. God only knows what she thinks. Again, I rub the shoulders of her red coat. Then I sit back in my seat, gaze out at the passing darkness. As I do, the film in my mind – the one where I am saved by Bob Hewitt – clicks vividly into action. But this time Bob doesn't star in it. It's someone else now, someone new to the rescue, someone very, very famous. That name, Cruise, I think to myself, Cruise, Cruise, where have I heard that before?

* * *

A new teacher arrived at my school. He was a fat, sweaty man with greased-back hair and an untidy appearance. His name was Mr Rawlings and he lived near Geoff Loughton in Camberley. One night he gave Geoff a lift home.

'It was hilarious,' Geoff told us the next day. I was listening but I wasn't hearing. 'On the way, he told me that he knew a lot of the local bus drivers. He used to work for the company or something. Said he was mates with all of them. So we're going along and every bus that drives past, he's going, oh look, there's Charlie or there's Bill or there's Alan and he's waving to them. And the funny thing is that all of these drivers are going past looking at him like he's a complete nutter. I don't think he knew any of them.'

For some reason, that morning in class, we moved in for the kill. It hadn't been discussed. It just happened. Every one of his questions was greeted with an abusive answer. Every demand of his was ignored. Geoff was the worst. He always was with the teachers. He viewed all of them with a surly contempt. With Rawlings, Geoff was in his element.

'Sir, is that your wig on the floor or has the hamster escaped from the science lab?'

'Sir, Teresa Driver just told me she fancies you. Do you fancy her?' Finally, Rawlings could take no more.

'Right, that's it,' he shouted and he dramatically threw his chalk onto the floor, 'I've had enough. You've killed me. I'm dead.'

He then fell to the floor as if a bullet had just flown through the window and lodged itself in his heart. There was a silence. Then we heard his voice from below.

'I'm dead, class. Well done, you've killed me.'

I couldn't help it. A smile cracked my misery in two. Better still, all of us in that class, every boy and every girl, started to laugh as one.

'Yeah, that's right. You go ahead and mock me,' we heard him shout from the floor, 'but I'll have the last laugh on you all. I will.'

'No, you won't, sir,' Geoff Loughton shouted back. 'You're dead.'

And in that shared laughter I buried my hurt and made myself believe that I didn't need a father.

* * *

I loved getting drunk. I loved the exhilaration it gave me. I liked the way it unlocked my inside, made me say things which previously I had kept under wraps. Drunk, I told mates about the girls I fancied at school and regretted doing so the next day. I told them about people I despised and regretted doing so the next day. Drunk, I was up for any caper. Drunk, I would argue like crazy. Drunk was generous. It gave me another world to inhabit, one in which I could do and say whatever I liked and damn tomorrow because drunk doesn't know tomorrow. Or the future. Or exams. Or jobs. Or adults who beat you and betray you. Drunk never has done and it never will. That is its power. Drunk only lives in the now. Of course, I hated drunk for making me sick and I hated drunk for the way it made the room whirl around me as I prayed for sleep. But on Friday nights, I was its friend again, eager to be with it. For I loved feeling out of control, out of this world. Loved it.

Most weekends, I stumbled home with friends, shouting, singing and cursing into the warm summer air, my stomach bloated with Watneys Ale. Inquisitive police cars would sidle up next to us. They would ask for names and I would quote Shakespeare at them. 'Blow thy cataracts, crack thy lightning.'

They would ask again and I would tell them my name was Pete Townshend.

'Well, get home now, Pete, before you spend the night in a cell.'

One time, Pete Garland and I were rushing down the high street in town. He was in a supermarket trolley and I was pushing it. He was yelping like a puppy and I was drunk. The cops pulled up. Two got out of the car.

'What's your name?' one of them asked me. 'Pete Townshend,' I replied.

He turned to Pete. 'What's yours?' 'Paolo Hewitt,' he replied.

Oh, I loved being drunk.

* * *

One day, as usual, I was in the playground playing life-and-death football. I hated losing, however trivial the game. Losing ruined everything for me. The playground was crowded with boys, darting here, running there, a mass of moving arms and legs and shouts and screams. In this game, we were two–nil down and I was fuming. In five minutes, the final bell for the afternoon lessons would go and it didn't look like we were ever going to score. Just then, the ball skidded away towards some second-year boys. I ran after it.

'Oi, mate,' I shouted, gesturing to a well-built second year for him to kick the ball back to me, 'over here.'

He was a big lad with a lumpy physique. He looked towards me and then, as the ball reached his foot, he kicked it as hard as he could and as far away from me as possible. Then he looked at me and he grinned.

I exploded. 'You want a fight, mate? Hey, wanker, want a fight?' 'Yeah,' he said and he walked towards me and threw a right-hand punch that caught me flush on the side of the head. Next thing I knew, he was all over me, his fists flying into my back, the weight of him impossible to manoeuvre around. He crushed me to the ground and, if the truth be told, I had no escape from this unexpected and vicious pummelling.

My boys rushed over and separated us, three of them pushing him away. Relief and pain and shame poured through me. I hadn't been able to throw one single punch. Most of the playground had watched. They had now received the message – that Paulo Hewitt, he ain't as tough as he makes out. That second year just beat him up. You're joking? No, it's true. A second year beat him up.

The story went round the school in an instant. For days I felt weak.

I took seven O levels and passed five. I could now stay on for A levels at school. Did I feel happy with myself, pleased as punch? No way. I failed two O levels; I didn't just pass five. That's how I thought. Anything to whip myself with, eh?

* * *

Pete Mac enters the back sitting room where cathode rays illuminate our shiny faces. He claps his hands together.

'Esther, Sarah, Ann – time for bed.'

Sarah and Ann, clad in their striped dressing gowns and slippers stand and say, 'Night, everyone.'

A low murmur of voices answers them. Esther doesn't move. She stays slumped on the sofa, staring at the television.

'Esther, I said bedtime.' Again, no movement. 'Esther.'

Still no movement. But a question, instead. 'Why do I have to go to bed?'

'Because it's your bedtime, that's why,' Pete Mac cheerfully replies. 'No, it's not.'

'Yes, it is.'

'No, it's not.'

'Don't argue with me, Esther.'

'Esther, do what Pete says.' This is Lynn, a new member of staff, talking. She arrived about a month ago. Two weeks later, Dominic, another staff member, arrived. The rumour is that they are having it off although no one seems quite sure. Meanwhile, Pete Mac is now seeing Julie. She left Barry and moved into her flat with Des but it hasn't even lasted six months. Des got bored and found someone else. Pete then bumped into Julie in town and one thing led to another. I was still seeing Rosie and Martin was still visiting Kim. Emily had left a few months back. When Rosie was asleep, I had thought a few times of going to Val's room and testing the waters there but I was prevented by the proximity of her room to Rosie's. Could be tricky. But not impossible.

'I'm older than those two,' Esther spat out, 'so why should I go to bed?'

This was true. Esther was twelve, Sarah and Ann were a couple of years younger. Unfortunately Esther shared the same room as them and so was put to bed at the same time so as not to disturb them. It was unfair, even more so when you're trying to watch *Are You Being Served?* and you know that at school on Monday everyone will be talking about it.

Esther didn't wait for a reply. She wanted to make another point. 'If I have to go to bed why doesn't David? He's the same age as me.'

'I'm not going to bed now,' David sullenly replied from his chair in the corner of the room. Like everyone else, his eyes were fixed on the screen.

'Oh look,' said Kim, 'the budgie has just died.' Kim often did this, verbally reacting to the action on the screen. 'Oh look,' she would say as we gazed at a film, 'he's shot her.' Or, 'Oh look, they've just kissed,' or 'Oh look, he's dead now.'

'That reminds me, David,' Pete said, 'you didn't clean the bathroom when I asked you.'

'What time is the football on?' I asked impatiently. It was a way of saving David, who was struggling for an answer, plus I hated early Saturday night TV. It was full of crappy game shows or light entertainment shows with singers in velvet jackets, their hair worn a little long on the collar as if to say, 'Yeah, I'm with it.' Or there were comedies like *Are You Being*

Served? which I thought just weren't funny. I could never lose myself in it like I could in *The Sweeney* or a book or a record.

'We're not watching football, are we?' Phil asked. He was sat next to me, another new recruit, another child of damage.

'Bloody are. And Parkinson.'

Parkinson, I liked. He was a suave man with sideburns, a great interviewer who somehow found the time to write a column on cricket for the *Sunday Times*. If I didn't make it as a music writer, I decided I would be him instead – rich and famous with a great job.

'Don't swear, Paulo,' Pete snapped, 'it's not clever.' 'Never said it was.'

'Esther, come on now, bedtime. David, Stephen, Billy, your turn in half an hour. Esther, I'm warning you…'

She rose slowly, her eyes still on the TV. 'Night, everyone,' she said sullenly. Another murmur of voices. Then we went back to watching Mrs Slocombe's pussy.

In the morning Pete walked into the back sitting room, pulled back the curtains and saw that Kim had been right all along. The budgie had died.

* * *

In the final class of the year, the teacher announced that the election of head boy for September would now take place. The class would make their nominations for the title and then we would all vote.

'Paulo Hewitt,' Vic said. There was a murmur of assent. I waited for other names to be put forward. None came. The teacher waited. I waited. Silence.

Then I understood. It was the boys' final gift to me before they left and finally entered the world they craved, the world of work and pubs and gassy beer and alarm clocks and stupid foremen and horrible bosses and dirty, grey sandwich-boxes and grease and paint and dirt and vans and cars and fights on Fridays and shags on Saturdays and football on Sundays and what do you know – a little money in your pocket for the week.

I never wanted to be head boy. How could I report to teachers about kids smoking out in the playing fields? I was that kid. Everyone knew it, from the headmaster down. I didn't even know if I was going to stay on at school. But as I sat there in that silence I felt truly moved by their action. It was indeed the boys' last gift to me and I loved them all for it. I really did. The piss-taking bastards.

She and I had finally got talking during these roller-coaster years of mine but it never led anywhere. Wherever we were, I always froze in her presence. She was beautiful and so sophisticated and She moved in waters I couldn't hope to swim in. We got to kiss once at a house party but, as I came to discover, the hope of the dream is always better than the truth of the moment. We never kissed again. And I liked it that way. We Catholics, lapsed or not, always need a Madonna in our lives.

* * *

That summer, one lunchtime, my social worker arrived and finally I went to meet my two half-sisters for the very first time. They both lived in the same town in Surrey. Nina was a housewife with two children, Suzie and Tanya. David, her

husband, worked on the stock market. Frankie, the younger
one, was married to Pete and had one daughter, Kay. Frankie
worked as a hairdresser. We were to meet at Nina's house.

My social worker drove and, on the way, we spoke about
my invisible father. She later wrote of the conversation, 'his
attitude on this occasion was how could he miss something
that he never had.'

I had done it. I had buried my feelings. I had dug the
grave and poured my hopes of ever knowing him into the
gaping hole I had created. Then I had covered these feelings
with earth – rich, thick, crumbly earth – and then walked
away. Never again, I decided, would I think of my father. It
was a strange feeling, finding close family at such a late stage
in life. Part of me felt there was no point to the meeting. The
other half of me was slightly intrigued to make contact.

It was early afternoon when we pulled up outside Nina's
place. They were waiting on the doorstep to greet us and as I
looked upon them for the very first time I was struck by the
difference between the two. Frankie was small. She wore her
brown hair shortish and it was a good cut, for it emphasised
her eyes. Nina was taller but skinnier and stood at the back
of the group. She seemed reserved in her greetings, happy
to let Frankie take charge. Even though they had grown up
together, first with our mother and then with a foster mother,
they had evolved into quite separate entities. Nina was now
extremely well-off; her house was large with a garden. Frankie
lived down the road in a much smaller abode. Nina was the
sensitive one, shy like me. She quizzed me on my studies,
my tastes in music, cinema and books. Frankie was down to
earth, straightforward. She gave her opinion and stood her
ground. Life for her was simple. It revolved totally round her
home. Their relationship intrigued me. As ever, I stayed quiet,

spoke when I was spoken to, raised no questions. Later in life, I would see that I was a mixture of them both.

My social worker sat in the background and when the conversation dried up she stepped in and brought a fresh impetus to the proceedings. It was a good start, it was an awkward start, it was a testing start. Above all, though, it was a start.

But one thing bothered me. As we drove away, I realised that none of us had mentioned our mother. Her name had not been raised; her life not examined. Both parties still saw her as theirs and theirs alone. That reality would take many years to crack. But crack it had to.

I would later discover that my sisters refused to acknowledge me when they were first told of my existence. They thought I was a cruel dream thought up by someone just to torment them. The fact that their mother, the one who had been so cruelly taken from them, could suddenly bear another child was beyond their reasoning. The one thing they could cling to – this is our mother and no one else's – had been taken from them. They forgot me as best they could and it took years for them to finally face me head on, to acknowledge me and then to hold out their hands to me. In doing so, they showed a small part of the beauty my mother gave us all.

I went to see my mother again that Christmas. It was the first time I had seen her since the revelation about my father had stoned me to my soul. I didn't say anything to her on the matter. I didn't have the language or the strength. I was polite, pleasant. I gave her a gold bracelet and she gave me a calendar. I threw it away when I got home. It wasn't a record or a book and so had no value to me. But I carried on seeing her.

In a year's time, I would sit with her and my social worker and my two sisters. We would drink tea and there would be silences and there would be some smiles but above all there would be a healing.

And sometimes in my dreams I see us in Sorrento. I dream I have just come round the corner and there is a basket hanging by a rope from a window really high above. It is the basket that the wives let down to the street and is filled with fruit and vegetables. But in the dream my mother and my two sisters stand inside it. They motion to me and I go and step inside that basket too. And we are pulled, all of us, towards the sky.

* * *

Questions were now being raised about my future. Would I stay on at school for A levels? Would I go on to work? Would I go to a technical college? I had no idea. One evening, I went for a drink down the pub we frequented. Pete Garland was there, among others. So was Little Willie. He was sitting in the corner surveying us. My heart sank as soon as I saw him. Little Willie was well known around town. He was seven foot tall with curly long hair and a scar that extended from his left eye down his cheek and then veered off towards his mouth. It was said that the group Sweet had written their song, 'Little Willie,' in his honour. It was said that one of the group members lived in a nearby village and had held a party one night. Little Willie came to that party and Little Willie refused to leave that party until he was good and ready. Thus the chart hit 'Little Willie (Won't Go Home)' had been born. I too had had a run in with him. One evening, I had been sat alone in the pub waiting for friends when he sat down next to me and said, 'Sniff this.'

I had no choice. I sniffed the small, dark bottle he had jammed under my nose. The world went upside down, round and round, all in twenty seconds. 'Did you like that?' he asked as I came back to earth.

'Yes,' I eagerly replied, wondering what the hell had just gone on. 'Good,' he said, 'because I am going to fuck you on it later.' Again, the world went upside down and round and round.

'Willie,' I said, gathering together my senses as quickly as I could, 'there's a record I want to put on the jukebox.'

'Okay,' he replied.

I stood, went to the jukebox by the front door, and I bolted out of that pub as fast as my legs could take me.

This was the first time I had seen him since that incident. Thankfully, his vision seemed so impaired by chemicals and alcohol, I don't think he recognised me. I got a drink and sat next to Pete. He was now working for an office equipment factory near his home. We spoke of football and The Who and these jazz guys he was listening to and what girls we fancied and suddenly I got drunk and told him of my dilemma about my future.

'See, I've got to leave the Home at some point. They kick you out when you're eighteen.'

'Simple,' he said, putting down his empty pint on the table. 'I'll have a word with my mum and dad. You can live with us. My sister Margaret has moved out so her room's free.'

The next day I received a letter. I had been accepted at a local technical college to study two A levels.

Rosie and I lie in bed for the last time. Neither of us says anything but we know our time is drawing to a close.

'Do you think I'm getting fat?' I ask her. Forever the worrier.

'Stop it,' she replies, rubbing her hands on my chest. 'I can feel your ribs from here. Fat – huh.' She puts her roll-up to her lips and she says, 'You'll visit, won't you?'

'Of course I will,' I say.

Rosie nods and then from under her pillow she hands me a book of poems, written by an Italian poet from the sixteenth century, in which the words glow like burning coal. They tell of a man's descent into hell but also of his rise and rise and rise into the light that belongs to each and every one of us. I stare at the book for a while, put it by the side of the bed and draw Rosie close to me.

And when I awake she has gone, disappeared into that very light.

They held a party for my leaving. They gave me a copy of The Who's Greatest Hits and all of us ate sausage rolls and some of us sneaked beer into our cups. Pete Mac made a speech and then hugged me. Later, he gave me his home phone number, and I use it to this day. Linda and Dom smiled at me indulgently and whilst I spoke to Agassi, Martin nicked a couple of fags out of her packet and we went outside.

'I don't know what the fuss is about,' I told him. 'I'll probably be back next week.' He was now working full-time at the antique shop and soon he would go and live above it. A year later and he too will have disappeared. 'Whatever happens to you,' he said, jabbing his fag at me, 'make some fucking money. It's the only way. Promise?'

'Yeah,' I said, 'I promise.' I never did but twenty-five years later I would finally know the wisdom of his words.

The next morning, I walked down the drive for the very last time as a looked after kid. Next to me were the gardens where I had learnt my football. Behind me was the Home where I had grown up, the place where my memories will live forever. I had tears in my eyes, that I cannot deny.

I got halfway down the drive when I heard a shout. I looked to my right and suddenly I saw myself flashing by on a bicycle, rushing towards the garden, twelve years old and about to leap into the air and feel freedom rush into my veins. A car horn sounds. I turn and a police car glides past and I see myself and Laz sitting in the back, glum and beaten. And all the way down the drive, upon the holly leaves that I have watched turn white with snow and back again for years and years, faces now magically appear, the faces of Barry and Julie and Rosie and Pete, and further along all the children, all the little looked after kids, the children big and small that I now know were my true family all along.

Their smiles make me swallow my tears and I walk through the gates with hope and a strange, rugged determination.

Eight

My Essential Tomorrow

1 September 2001

I arrive at George's house to watch the football, Germany versus England, the famous 2001 World Cup qualifier. Chris, his brother-in-law, is there, so is David who works with him.

'Come on the Germans,' I say, settling into my seat. David, a Scotsman, looks at me quizzically.

'Why don't you support England?' he asks.

Damn. The Saturday-night question has arrived, and quicker than usual.

'Because my mother is Italian.' 'What's your father?'

'English,' I reply, instantly lying through my teeth. As soon as I let go of that answer, I am kicking myself.

'Well, why don't you support England?'

I know David and I like him but I don't know him well enough to spill the beans. Even George, one of my closest friends for years now, is unaware of the real story. He's looking a little uneasy at this exchange. Why don't you support England? Such a simple question to ask but such an impossible one to answer.

Perhaps I should have explained. Perhaps I should have told David that I have always supported Italy because that is the only part of me I know to be true. I don't know the other half of me. I also support Italy for my mother who died five years ago – in the nursing home they had placed her in once the hospital was closed down by the then Tory government.

She lasted about two years there. I visited her there about four times a year with my sisters. She remained the same. She kept quiet, made no friends, went to bed early. But she was proud of me. Nina or Frankie had shown her one of my articles in the music paper I worked for and she loved it.

'So many words, Paolo,' she cooed, 'so many words.'

Then she giggled. I can still hear and see that giggle. After she was buried, I took her ashes home. Later on, I packed them in a bag and I took them to Sorrento. One summer's night, with my beloved close by, I took them down to the bay of Napoli and I sprinkled them into the dark waters. The next day, I sent a postcard to my sisters. I wrote, 'Our mother is finally home.'

I feel closer to my mother now, now that I understand her life and her pain. Sometimes, as I walk down grey streets or stare out of frosty windows, I will look upwards and talk to her, ask her advice. We get closer with each passing day.

I wish she could have taught me Italian. I daydream about being brought up a son of Sorrento. It hurts that I can't speak their language and don't know their customs, their way of life. Even now, the pull of Italia remains strong. When I was twenty I was sent there to interview a rock group called The Clash. I will always remember stepping off that plane and immediately feeling that I was home. That feeling, so strong and vital in its nature, seemed to illuminate my whole being.

I have clung hard to that in me which is Italian. It is hardly surprising. The fact remains that I do not know my father and therefore I do not know the other half of me. The fact remains that in my life I have been stripped of my country, my birthright, my class. Even my name was stolen from me. It meant that for years I struggled to find my identity, to find out who I really was and where I was meant to be going. Italy was the only real thing I could grasp onto as that search for the inner man began, and so I grasped it hard.

And, lest you think it, I am not anti-British. I feel a true affinity with the working-class of this land. I love their clever nature, their taste in music and clothes, their wit and humour, and, above all, their compassion. I love this country's music and many of its artists. What I despise is this country's class system and the games you are meant to play to further yourself.

I hate the fact that I am judged by my accent and not my talent. I hate the island mentality and the Royal Family. And I can never forget what this country did to my mother. But I love London and I love my life and I am proud of my achievements. Until my drive to succeed wanes, it is here that I will stay. Although somebody, at some point, should do something about the weather.

Anyway, there is one other fact I forgot. Given the footballing skill, style and success of both nations, if you were given the choice of supporting either England or Italy, which one would you take?

I couldn't tell David all this. But now I can.

The next day I walk into a park and stand still and motionless under a cold blue sky. In front of me, lines of grey concrete cut through the beguiling green of the park. Ahead of me a church spire points upwards to what it believes is the answer. A noise from above attracts my attention and I look up to see a plane, probably finally making its way home from the '60s.

I am forty-three years old. I am the author of ten books. I am financially challenged and still a worrier. I worry about my weight, my looks, my intelligence. I worry about my friends and I worry about the world. Yet despite this habit of a lifetime, spiritually I am on the up. When I awake, most mornings I smile at myself in the mirror. My life is populated with great people. I am lucky. I am moving towards a peace within myself.

It has not been easy. More and more, as I look back over my years, especially my twenties, I see how unhappy I truly was. At the time, I denied it. I told myself I was right and the rest of the world was wrong. Now I am not so sure. Now when I look back, I see how in London, the city of my refuge, I took out my revenge on people, most of them women and girls. I used them badly. I took what I could from them and then in the morning I ran. I let them get close and then I snapped them in half, left them broken just as the world had broken Mrs K. and just as the world had broken my mother. I told them nothing of my past but I promised them all my future. Until they had done my bidding. Which was when I cast them aside, like empty sweet papers. My blood runs cold sometimes when I think of some of my behaviour at that time. And so the wheel of misfortune keeps on turning. I say again, people beware the unhappy for theirs is the sweetest revenge of all.

With others, I kept my distance. I let few get close. My shyness was mistaken for arrogance. My name was blackened by many. I didn't care.

I sought a million ways to soothe my pain. I was eager for medication. I still am. I am not totally out of the forest of confusion. I still have days where depression and a bitter anger makes me hate everyone in the world. I still have days where inside my mind I curse everyone, even my loved ones.

I still have these feelings because I have not rid myself yet of the cruel voice that lives inside me, which tells me that I need no one, that I can trust no one; that I should be alone because no one cares about me, because everyone is a liar and a cheat.

But that cruel voice is wrong and those days are now the exception, not the rule. Most of my time I gasp at the beauty of this world and am touched by the human kindness and care shown towards me. Most days, I am happy to be alive, to be working, thinking, loving, playing. Most days are good and some have been utterly fantastic. I am moving towards the light. I see the value of love. Now, I want to live in it.

Forever.

I start walking across the park. As I do, a thought quietly explodes inside my head. You know something, Paolo?

What?

It really is about time you found your father.

Epilogue
In the Land of Might-Have-Beens
January 2002

This book allowed me to arrive at a certain truth. It took three years to write and a million years to prepare. Throughout that time, I experienced lengthy bouts of real self-doubt as I wondered just what I was doing laying bare my life for all the world to see. Writing is a hard enough job to begin with. Adding real misgivings to the equation cruelly doubles the load. It was only when I had decided to delete every word I had written to date that two events occurred to forcefully convince me otherwise.

The first sign took place on the day I appeared on the LND radio station talking about a new book of mine entitled *The Soul Stylists*. The interview took place in the morning and by lunchtime I was home. I had not been writing long when the phone rang. It was the radio station saying that just after I had left a Joy Baltimore had called and left her number. Could I call her?

My heart skipped a beat when I heard the name. Joy Baltimore. Mio Dio. I hadn't seen Joy in twenty years, although she could never vacate my memory. Joy was my social worker during the teenage years I spent in the children's Home. Throughout my time in care I had other social workers but Joy was always my favourite. Not only did I have a slight fancy for her at the age of fourteen but she and I got on well. She knew books, knew a little music, knew a little cinema – but more than that, I always felt that, unlike many of the others, she was genuinely interested in my past, present and future.

Her actions often matched her words. As our relationship progressed, Joy had set about reuniting my broken family with a quiet determination. She made no big promises about doing so but laid the ground for my blood family to finally come together. She plays an important part within our fractured history.

After I left the Home, we drifted out of contact. It was a shame but it was the way of these things. No one was to blame. I was soon living in London and busy finding my way, finding myself. I was studying at college but was also writing part-time for a music paper. This was the start of my dream being realised. My mind was focused on the now. No time for looking back.

In fact, I now see that I was desperate to bury my past. That wasn't surprising. I had been beaten at seven, abandoned at ten and spent much of my teenage years slumped in dark depressions. London gave me the chance to make myself anew. In the capital, I could forget my past, reinvent it even. London, after all, is where everyone comes to bury their secrets. I was no different. I was eager to move forward. But to do so I had to shake off those behind me. Unfortunately Joy and her husband Tim became part of my culling. I rarely rang her after moving to London although I did occasionally think of her and when I did I kicked myself for not keeping in touch. Now, some twenty years later, I had the chance to bring her back into my life.

I called the number she had left. She answered the phone herself. We exchanged excited pleasantries and then she said, 'Do you know how I found you, Paolo? I got in my car this morning and turned on the radio expecting to hear Radio Four. That's the station I always have on. I don't listen to anything else. But the dial was set to another station. One of my kids had used the car and listened to another station. So I start flicking through the dial to get it back to Radio Four and as I'm flicking that's when I heard your name on the radio.'

'Joy,' I replied, 'you don't know this but I am currently writing a book about my past. I have been writing it for what seems like forever and right now I am at the stage where I first meet you. And look at that – bang, you come back into my life.'

'I'm not that surprised,' she simply said.

We arranged a meeting. Lunch on a Friday, Soho, London. An Italian restaurant, her treat. During the course of that meal, I expressed to Joy my desire to look at my social work files. These are the documents that are kept on you whilst you are in care. They contain reports of visits made by your social workers, comments from staff members at the Home, details of discussions held concerning your future. In 1977, the then Labour Government gave 'looked after kids,' as they are now called, the right to look at their files. I had already written to the Social Services asking to see mine. Some guy whose name I forget called me back. He said he was going on holiday but would track them down on his return – promise. (As I still haven't heard from him, I presume he is still looking. If it is of any help, mate, they are in the drawer marked 'Case Studies.')

When I told Joy I wanted to see my files, she gently smiled.

She said, 'I don't know if you remember but when you were fourteen or fifteen, I temporarily left you. I had to go to America for a year and study.'

'Of course. And Julia Lindsay then became my social worker for a year. I liked Julia a lot.'

'Well, Julia now works in the office where your files are kept.'

A month later, at Christmas, we all met at a Surrey pub. Julia had found my files, all three bulging folders. But first she and Joy wanted to warn me of what to expect. Going through this stuff will hit you in ways you don't even realise, they told me. 'You are about to confront a past that is extremely painful and reading this material will bring back feelings you thought were over. On top of that you are going to have to be ready to find things in there that you might not know about at the moment. Such information could well knock you for six.'

Typical, I thought. Twenty years down the line and these two women were still looking out for me.

I told them my position. I had had enough of my past dictating my present and future. I had had enough of my past making me feel low, insecure and frightened. I had to face up to it. I was getting close to the point where I had more years behind me than in front of me. It was time to take on, as best I could, the demons I'd lived with for what seemed like forever.

I said all this with genuine force and conviction and prayed to God that they hadn't noticed the tears welling up behind my eyes, like a dam ready to burst. I have a terrible fear of breaking down in public. Who knows what it might lead to.

In January, March and May, I made three visits to Julia's office to read my files. Joy stayed with me the whole time, Julia when she could.

I began to read and re-read the story of my life. It was an amazing experience. In those files you see and hear people talking about your character, your appearance, your demeanour. You see how others view you. Your reactions to events are recorded and so is your world view. Not only is your early life set down forever but also chronicled are the memories that will never fade and the ones that already have. I think it is the closest you can get to attending your own funeral – which makes it a one-off experience, one of the very few perks of being a looked after kid. Most people don't have such files. They have photograph albums. We have brown files and these mark us out from the crowd. But, as with all such situations, there is a price to pay.

Joy and Julia were spot on. In reading this material I once again keenly felt those feelings of isolation and abandonment that had ruined my childhood. I forced myself to see how love had been denied me, how I had been stripped of everything, even my proper name. I felt again the violence of my foster mother; recalled the dark days I lived, filled with a heavy, quiet despair and nothing else. This when I was but seven years old. Re-connecting with such awful feelings hit me hard. They will stay with me for a long time. But that's part of the journey, part of the struggle I knew I was getting into. Even so, I was still unsure about setting it all down in a book. Despite Joy's reappearance in my life, doubts still crowded around my heart. Then came the second event, the second sign convincing me.

When my foster mother let me go I was placed in a Home called Woodrough. I was ten years old at the time. According to my files it states that at Woodrough I became very friendly with one Adrian Brown, the son of John and Molly Brown, the kindly couple who ran Woodrough. During that next week, I thought of Adrian a lot, tried to recall his face and manner. Yet my mind's eye remained blank when it came to him, although it easily recalled many others. For instance, I had no problem remembering John and Molly Brown. They treated me with such huge kindness. So it surprised me that I could not recall their son. Try as I might, I simply couldn't place him. One Monday morning, I checked my e-mails. There was one from my publishing company. It said simply, 'We have received the following e-mail and have passed it on to you. Hope you're well.'

I opened it. The first sentence read, 'I don't know if you are the Paolo Hewitt who was at Woodrough Children's Home in 1968 but my name is Adrian Brown...' Adrian now worked in Amsterdam. He made musical instruments for a living. He was in London on business and happened to turn on the television when a Rod Stewart documentary was being shown. I was on that documentary and Adrian had recognised me from it. He had then gone onto the internet and discovered who had published my last book.

I couldn't believe it. I got in touch with Adrian and we wrote to each other with a growing sense of excitement. It was he who sent me the beautiful photograph that adorned the cover of the first edition of this book. From that point onwards, all my doubts about writing the book were crushed. If that wasn't enough, Julia Lindsay gave me a further motive. 'Paolo,' she said to me during that pub lunch, 'I always say to people if you are dealt a lemon in life, make lemonade.' I loved that. This book, then, is my bottle.

With my mind now free of worry I came to realise that I was writing this book for many different people. I was writing it for my mother whose life was so harsh upon her and I was writing it for my two half-sisters, Frankie and Nina. I was writing it for my second family, the one made up of the friends who have helped me so much along my path with their shouts of encouragement and their declarations of love. But most of all I felt as if I was writing it for the kids in my Home and for the thousands of us whose lives, through no fault of our own, have been made hell by the hate and cruelty of others.

I came to London at nineteen years of age with nothing. No family, no money, no country, no class. My dream was to write for the music paper, the *New Musical Express*. At twenty-four, I realised that dream. Through that job I travelled the world, interviewed musicians such as Marvin Gaye, Stevie Wonder, Nina Simone and others whose work still gets me through the dark hours.

But all the time I was there, there was a voice inside my head that cruelly mocked my success. It said, the only reason you were given this job was because someone found out you were from a Home and took pity on you. You have no talent, no merit. You just have someone who took pity on you.

I gave into that voice far too many times and thus I never fully enjoyed the job I had spent so much time yearning for. It was only after I had left the *NME* and strangers would come up and shake my hand for the pleasure my work had given them that I learnt that nobody hurts you harder than yourself.

I wasn't without talent. I just had a bad case of luck, simple as that. At the start of my life, an unbalanced woman whose own childhood had been one of severity and mental cruelty entered my life. I lived in a nursery at the time. If I had been taken out that afternoon or if someone else had walked in half an hour earlier and taken a shine to me, my life would have been completely different. It could either have been absolutely joyful or else even worse than it proved to be. Such is life and how luck plays such a heavy part in fighting its uncertain, uncontrollable nature.

My foster mother's humiliation of me as a child meant that for many years I felt as if I was nothing more than a dead flower being blown from one barren field to another, forced there by unstoppable cruel winds. I don't feel that way now. I got lucky. I was put into care and during those years certain people, members of staff and kids, carried me through.

I went to school and found a great bunch of friends. I left school and came to London. There, I forged links with people who I will hold hands with when we jump into the next world. Of course, if someone had come along to me when I was a child whose every day filled him with absolute fear, and said, 'Look, I know it is hard to believe but trust me, there is love in this world and it can be yours, it doesn't have to be the dark place you think it to be, it can actually be the most magical place imaginable,' I would have laughed bitterly in their face. But love has now changed me. So has time. Now I want a life. Now I feel I have a lot of catching up to do.

There is never any closure for the extreme pain that is heaped upon children such as myself, one of the unlucky ones. There is never any true 'getting away' from the nightmare of your past. It hovers at the back of your mind, an uneasy guest amidst all the traffic flowing in and out. Sometimes you can ignore it, other times the weight drags you down to places no one should go. But there is a light in this world that can keep it at bay. It is made from pure love and you can live in it. It will give you strength, it will give you hope, it will give you courage, it will give you belief and one day – and I know I would never have believed this in a million years – you will find that you can actually shine it on others. If you get the chance to do so, don't let it pass you by.

'My Future' by Paul K.

(Written aged ten, at Staines Preparatory School)

When I grow up I want to be an actor, but my teacher says it is very difficult to be an actor, as I am not getting on at all well at this school – I must pull myself together.

First of all I want to work to pass my 11 plus, then if I want to go on to a grammar school I want to pass my Common Entrance. I then want to get about five O levels and three A levels. I then want to get married and if possible get some children. I then want to get a job as an actor.

So far I am not getting on very well at Staines, I have had the cane and also three 'cards' and a lot of detentions. If I fail to be an actor I will either try to be a rugby, cricket or football player. It is quite hard to be either of these, but I will still try.